Acclaim for Your Family Needs You

"I am so happy Mervin has written this. It can act as a blueprint and reference point for the toughest job in the world - Parenting."

EDDIE NESTOR MBE (TELEVISION AND RADIO PRESENTER)

"Your Family Needs You is a powerful and thoughtful examination of the family unit in all its facets - good bad, ugly, joyful and necessary. Mervin Cato writes with refreshing honesty and authenticity taking his life experiences as his own personal journey into the study of the value of the family unit. It is a great read with a powerful message."

NITIN GANATRA OBE (ACTOR)

"...If you do not have a better insight to yourself and the world around you after reading this book then I really don't know what else to say!"

HON DR STUART LAWRENCE (ACTIVIST, AUTHOR, CONSULTANT, YOUTH ENGAGEMENT SPECIALIST)

"With practical advice, and real-life experience, this book teaches the reader how, against the odds, they can build a strong family, a supportive community, and take full advantage of their education. This thoroughly enjoyable and entertaining book is a must read for all professionals in education or health and social care, especially those working with young people within deprived communities."

TOMMY OFFE – INVOLGIZE.COM (INTELLIGENCE THOUGHT LEADER)

"...a fantastic, vital, necessary, important book for everybody. An amazing piece of work. So many people I would like to give this book to!"

LINDSEY COULSON (ACTRESS)

"… really inspiring and full of golden nuggets that you can easily implement into your life & that of your children. I wish I had read this before my children reached their 30s!"

SARAH MOORE (GEE STAR PRODUC-TIONS)

"In a world filled with broken families this book is a breath of fresh air as well as a practical powerful guide to cultivating an environment in which to raise children who are healthy and whole. As a single mother of five who has often questioned whether or not I am 'getting it right', Mervin's writing style and his ability to keep it real and relatable helped me to feel as though I am not alone. I absolutely loved it!"

KAREN ALLEN (AUTHOR)

Your Family Needs You

Mervin Cato

Incorplus Publishing

Typeset in Garamond 14pt

ISBN: 978-1-0687532-6-8 (Paperback)

ISBN: 978-1-0687532-5-1 (Hardback)

ISBN: 978-1-0687532-7-5 (E- book)

A CIP Catalogue record for this book is available from the British Library

Unless otherwise indicated, all Scripture quotations are taken from the HOLY BIBLE, NEW INTERNATIONAL VERSION®

For Mum and Dad

Seven things this book will help you attain

1. Practical tips for managing family relationships and creating a positive home environment.

2. How to establish and reinforce positive values within your family.

3. Ways to build a strong support system to help you and your family navigate challenges.

4. Techniques for fostering honest and open conversations with your family.

5. Tools for understanding your own parenting style and its impact on your family.

6. Strategies to support your child and adding value to their personal growth, present and future.

7. How to effectively communicate with and collaborate with your child's school.

Contents

Foreword

I have always had an earnest belief that the family is the bedrock of society. Over centuries, there has been significant change in the family dynamic.

How modern society views the family and how 'family values' coexist with societal change, exemplifies the need to give this fundamental area of our lives, the due care and attention it deserves.

Your Family Needs You calls us to do exactly that. Mervin has stripped back and demystified, myths and traditions about key family challenges, principles and dynamics. Mervin has shared his life experience, faith and beliefs to help us better understand and appreciate both the obvious and subtle variations of family life.

The book has a great balance of stories, anecdotes, guidance notes and references to give practical advice on how to navigate the sometimes complex terrain of family life. I am sure this book will stir up some deep-rooted thoughts, feelings and emotions. It certainly did for me! It also provoked that key question that challenges us in life - what can I do differently?

Mervin, thank you for being obedient to the higher calling, thank you for being vulnerable and being prepared to open up some old wounds, thank you for being so transparent, and thank you for letting us know more about your remarkable family.

You remind me of Joshua in the Old Testament – 'but as for me and my house, we will serve the Lord' (Joshua 24 v15)

Anthony Williams – Regional Director of Education (OCL)

Preface

It's not uncommon to hear parents describe parenthood as a battle. A battle against sleepless nights, tantrums, and the endless demands of raising children. But for me, the analogy of parenthood to warfare is more than just a figure of speech. It's a reflection of the experiences I've witnessed, particularly in my mother's life.

The title of this book, "Your Family Needs You," is a direct reference to the iconic World War I recruitment poster featuring Lord Kitchener, the British Secretary of State for War. The poster, with its stern gaze and the powerful message "Your Country Needs You," became a symbol of national duty and sacrifice.

While the context is different, the sentiment behind the poster resonates deeply with the challenges and responsibilities of parenthood. Just as Lord Kitchener urged men to join the fight for their country, I believe that parents are called to defend and protect their families.

My mother's life was a testament to this idea of 'fighting for family'. She faced numerous challenges with us, from financial hardship to health issues. But despite these obstacles, her faith in God was a cornerstone of her strength and resilience. Her belief in God provided her with unwavering hope, even in the face of adversity. She often found solace and guidance in her prayers, drawing strength from her spiritual connection.

Mum and Dad remained steadfast in their commitment to their family. They fought tirelessly to provide for us, to ensure we had a safe and loving home, and to instil in us the values that would shape our lives.

Her battles were not fought on a physical battlefield, but in prayer. She fought against fear, uncertainty, and the constant threat of adversity. She strategized, planned, and made sacrifices, much like a general leading an army. Her determination and resilience were inspiring, and they taught me valuable lessons about the importance of family and the strength that comes from unity.

Parenthood, like warfare, requires a strategic approach. Parents must be prepared to face unexpected challenges, to adapt to changing circumstances, and to make difficult decisions. They must also be willing to sacrifice their own needs and desires for the sake of their family.

By adopting a strategic mindset and applying the principles in this book, parents can better equip themselves to navigate the complexities of family life and help their families flourish.

Introduction

Let me tell you a story about me.

I am 19 years old, a young roughneck on the streets of North London and I am an addict—addicted to the **Big L: Learning**. I was good at it but unfortunately, I was learning all the wrong things.

What I had learnt was that money came easily if you knew what to do, and I had no hesitation in learning what I needed to do. I was still living at home and a situation occurred where I made a big mistake in my house. My mum found out and her course of action changed my life.

The incident caused my mum to phone the police and I was arrested. The interview at the police station was traumatic, and given that my mum reported me, I had no option but to plead guilty.

Wood Green Crown Court is an intimidating place, and standing in the dock and being sentenced was devastating. Luckily for me, I did not get a custodial sentence, but my life changed forever. Not only did I now have a criminal record, but on my return to the family home in Edmonton, I was told by my dad that I needed to move out immediately. I was at rock bottom and did not know where to turn. Shunned by my family and on the streets, things could not have been worse. My life was over... at 19.

Rewind my selector!

Let's go back two paragraphs to the sentence that states: **My mum found out and her course of action changed my life.**

Well, what really happened was she looked at me and I looked at her and I asked her if she had found something out. She replied that she had, and then she turned and walked away. And that was the end of that. Not another word was mentioned. Ever.

My mum didn't even tell my dad (more about him later in the book). I know that is true because if she had, I would have been gone. There was me thinking at the age of 19 that my mother really didn't know me... well, I got that wrong. She did, and she must have analysed the bigger picture in this situation and decided the best thing to do was nothing, which saved me.

This was the first time I was conscious of parenting skills, of knowing your children and what is best for them. Don't get me wrong, I didn't immediately become an angel. My roughneck ways continued for a few more years, but I realised I had dodged a bullet and trod more carefully from that moment on. The decision my mum made that day altered the rest of my life.

Often in life you are faced with a choice of pathways, and success and failure are dependent on which you choose. That day, my mum made a parenting choice and I would not be in the place I am today if she had chosen differently, both in my personal as well as my professional life.

So, why have I decided to write this book? Well, like most people when they get over the age of 50, they have seen, smelt, tasted, touched, and heard so much. I want to share with you what my five senses have witnessed and experienced in relation to parents and parenting. The lessons I have learned and, more importantly, the mistakes I have made. One constant in my life has been that the best learning opportunities come from the mistakes and failures. This book comes from my heart in the vain hope that it can help at least one family and hopefully more. If I can achieve that, then 'job well done!'

Making intentional decisions for your family shouldn't be off the cuff—they should be planned and focused on a bigger picture or aspirations for your family. Hopefully, this book will help you on your family's journey to achieve this. And remember, **Life Long Learning** is the key.

Chapter One

Changing of a Culture

I am a husband, I have a lovely wife named Sophia and we have three wonderful children—Wesley, 28, Hannah, 21, and Helena, 17. Wesley has also made us proud grandparents of two great boys. Wesley has a different mother from his sisters as he was from a previous relationship. His mother and I split up when he was just one year old, however, I was able to have him most weekends if not every other weekend when he was younger.

When Wesley was around 13 years old, he was really struggling at school with his behaviour and attendance, which led to me getting constant calls from his mum wanting me to reprimand him. Discussions started about him possibly coming to live with me permanently and attending the school I was working at.

I was head of the behaviour unit at a secondary school in Enfield. Yes, I did say "behaviour unit", and there was my son having issues at his school and giving his mum a hard time at their home. He wasn't only misbehaving at school and with his mother, but now the bad behaviour had spilled over to my home and most of it was focused at his seven-year-old younger sister, Hannah.

When Wesley and Hannah were slightly younger, they had a great relationship. We have footage of them singing and dancing together - what happy siblings they were. But somewhere along the line, that had changed. What changed exactly? Well, a few things. Wesley's mum met someone else and he moved into their household. This really didn't go down well with Wesley as it had been just him and his mother living together for over 13 years. The other thing, according to Wesley, was at the time, his little sister, Hannah, was turning into this know-it-all—a smart-ass annoying little sister. I can't even lie, I could see it myself.

Most working people normally look forward to weekends, however, Sophia and I started to dread them. Wesley and Helena - his youngest sister – would gang up on Hannah on a regular basis. What I found strange was that if you didn't get on with someone then you didn't talk to them or go near them, right? I mean Wesley even had a separate room. But no, the children loved being in the same space, getting on each other's nerves. They were constantly bickering and then getting physical. Usually, it would be Hannah running to me crying, asking me to tell off Wesley and Helena, then Wesley and Helena would be pleading their case that it was all Hannah's fault. It was nonstop all weekend and even when we went out.

I remember us all going on a family camping trip—wow, what memories we have from that. We all laugh about it now, but at the time, it was sticks and spiders being thrown at each other and stag beetles mysteriously ending up in sleeping bags.

We have been on a few holidays over the years, however everyone remembers this one for all the wrong reasons.

Our children were terrorising each other.

It came to a head one rainy Saturday afternoon. Sophia went out with Helena, and I was in the front room with Wesley and Hannah. I was watching TV and Wesley started teasing his little sister as normal and then Hannah started to verbally defend herself. I thought, I'm just going to ignore this as I had used this tactic on a few occasions and sometimes it actually worked. Not this time! The bickering started to get louder and louder, and then Wesley hit Hannah. She started screaming - not that she was hit hard, but I guess Hannah wanted to catch my attention and get her brother into as much trouble as possible.

At that moment, I'd had enough. My patience was gone and I really just wanted to let my frustration out. Wesley was right by the front window and I stood up and was ready to give him a slap, but just as I opened my hand, I saw a figure outside on the road looking into our house. Was it a woman or an angel? To this day I'm not sure, but it was like she just stood there watching me and I froze and then she walked on.

I knew from that moment something seriously had to change. I mean, it doesn't sound great, does it? The head of a school behaviour department, absolutely losing it to the point that he wanted to hit his own son?

I'm of West Indian heritage and my dad was a very strict man. He and mum had 11 children together and, put it this way... my dad had his own way of parenting. This came from his roots in Jamaica so he most probably parented the same way as his father. How else was he going to manage 11 energetic children? So, I had a lot of experience of what hitting a child looked and felt like - but from the receiving end.

I don't know what things would have been like if I had hit Wesley that day as I was very angry and fed up, but that "angel" stopped me in my tracks. When I became a dad, I was determined not to repeat what mine had done – and there was I nearly doing exactly what I never wanted to ever do. It was a loud wake-up call that something had to be different.

About three weeks before this incident, I had attended a training session at my school. It covered many of the methods and behaviour techniques I already knew about, however, right at the end, they showed us an action plan technique for individual wellbeing. This plan was called: **STOP, START, CONTINUE**.

The method was all about committing your thoughts in writing. Things you wanted to **STOP** doing that weren't good for you, like smoking, spending a long time on the phone, spending loads of money on clothes, etc. Then writing down things you wanted to **START** doing like exercise, budgeting, eating healthy food, etc. Then finally writing down things that you were already doing that was good for you, which you wanted to **CONTINUE**. These then all had to be discussed with everyone at the meeting.

I decided that I was going to have a family meeting and incorporate an adapted version of this **STOP, START, CONTINUE** method to suit my family. I had chaired a great many meetings with families at work and seen some major break-throughs during these meetings, however, I had also seen the opposite where there was no agree-ment and the family remained divided. Did we ever do something like this when I was a child living with my parents? No way, no how! My dad just told us what to do and we had to do it with no discussion at all. Only one voice mattered and that was his.

It can be scary relinquishing control, allowing other opinions into the mix, but I decided the risk was worth taking for the sake of my family's well-being. Something had to change as the status quo was simply not working.

Sophia and I discussed my idea and she was in agreement that we should try it. We decided that we were going to allow everyone in the meeting to be equal and that no one would get into trouble for saying anything negative about someone if it wasn't intentionally meant to hurt them. We were going to focus on the behaviour, not the person. We also agreed to have the meeting at a time when it was relatively peaceful, and not right after an argument or a bickering session. We wrote out some basic rules—one person speaking at a time, no talking over each other, and whatever we discussed stayed in the house between us.

So, the big day came and the atmosphere seemed calm enough. It was a Sunday early afternoon and we wanted to give ourselves enough time so I could drop Wesley home after to prepare himself for school in the morning. I asked everyone to go to the back room where we had the dining table.

I started.

'We are going to have a family meeting where everyone can say what is really on their minds. No one will be in trouble for saying things as long as you say it in a nice way, and we are all on the same level in this meeting, including me and Mum. What we are going to use to help us is this paper.' I had five sheets of A4 paper with **STOP, START, CONTINUE** written at the top of each sheet in a landscape format.

'You can either write down what you would like to **STOP, START, CONTINUE** or what you would like someone else in this family to **STOP, START, CONTINUE**. Once everyone has finished, we will have a discussion and set some family targets. Helena, Mum will help you to write your ones down. Is everyone OK with this?' All three of them were nodding in silence. It was like they couldn't believe this was really happening. To be honest, it did seem a bit surreal. There was complete silence and everyone just seemed really mature at that moment—a rare event in our house.

I thought the first part would take two to three minutes max, but seven minutes went by and heads were still down. I was always told by Wesley's teachers that he was lazy, but for this, he was very engaged and totally focused. In my head, I had no doubt our children were writing things down about each other and having personal digs, and I was just preparing myself for working things out in an amicable way so that they all would be as happy as possible.

As Sophia was helping Helena, she was the last one to finish. I started reading out the meeting rules and letting them know we were going to discuss what we had written.

'Okay, who wants to go first and talk about their first **STOP**?'

'I will,' said Wesley. 'Dad, will you stop coming into my bedroom without knocking on the door?'

I was stunned—paralyzed like I had just been bitten by a dangerous insect from the depths of a jungle. I wanted to say, "Who do you think you're talking to? Who do you think pays the bills in this house? I can go into any room I want!"

But, rules are rules and I had to stick by them, but needless to say, I was fuming.

The idea should have been that I would reply to Wesley with an answer and then read out something I wanted him to **START** and we would trade off, but I was so shocked that I didn't know what to say. Thankfully, Sophia stepped in and asked if anyone else wanted to go next? Helena said, "Me, me, me!" As she was jumping on her seat, I just gave her the nod as I was still in shock mode. "Dad, can you stop shouting at us? You're angry all the time."

Wow, if Wesley had me on the ropes, then this was definitely the finisher. (Note: I love boxing and boxing references. I used to box when I was in school and it helped me a lot.) If you ever get a chance, go on YouTube and look at my favourite boxer, Big George Foreman. Type in Boxing Knockouts: George Foreman knocks out Gerry Cooney and look at the last two punches of the fight. George stuns Cooney with a big right and knocks him out with the left. Well, that's what it felt like—like I was knocked out by my children by a George Foreman style punch.

Thankfully, we were able to get through the meeting in the end. Sorry, let me rephrase that... I was just about able to survive the meeting in the end. It was evident, particularly from Wesley's sheet, that most of his frustration was with me and he had been taking it out on Hannah.

Everyone had written down their **STOP, START & CONTINUEs** and even though everyone had a few and we read them all out individually, we decided to action only two points from each person, and agreed which ones we wanted to trade off.

It took longer than we thought it would, but everyone was engaged. I typed up the master family copy and put it on the fridge for everyone to see.

Well, the question was, did it work? Yes, it definitely did work! The first six weeks were a dream, a total transformation.

For me personally, I got to know a lot about what Wesley was going through and I really focussed on being able to communicate with him to the point he could share most stuff with me. It was really the start of my relationship with Wesley taking a turn for the better.

I realised that a family doesn't just work automatically; things need to be in place and sometimes you need to take a leap of faith and take a risk.

LEARNING

Family Master Copy:

STOP	START	CONTINUE
Dad: Going into Wesley's room without knocking on the door	Wesley: Putting out the bins before leaving on Sunday night	Watching football together
Dad: Shouting	Helena: Tidying up after playing with her toys	Reading bedtime stories
Wesley: Picking on Hannah	Hannah: Calling Wesley by his proper name	Helping Helena with her words
Hannah: Correcting Mum all the time	Mum: Bringing Hannah to museums	Having conversations about school
Mum: Nagging	Helena: Respecting Hannah	Running in the park
Family: Stop family arguments	Family: Inviting other family members to the restaurant with us	Having family time games
		Having family meetings

Why not have a go at **STOP, START, CONTINUE** and see if that improves things in your family? By me and my wife empowering our children, by listening to their voices, we were able to change our family dynamic for the better.

Please feel free to introduce it to your family the way I did and see it transform your home.

Chapter Two

Wait Till Your Father Gets Home

I've mentioned it before, but my mother had 11 children with my dad, and even though everyone never lived in our three-bedroom house altogether at the same time, there was still at least seven or eight of us, plus my mum and dad at any one time, and that was plenty.

However, there were many advantages to this. If someone put a can of drink in the fridge and you drank it and the owner questioned whether you drank their drink or not, you just blamed someone else. That someone would then just blame someone else and so on. You could never run out of suspects! I was smart enough to have special hiding places all around the house for my food and drink so they rarely got taken.

We had loads of fun and lots of memories living as a big family in a relatively small house. The main disadvantage was privacy because there was none. I always shared a bedroom with my brothers. The boys' room was the smallest bedroom in the house, and we had a double bunk bed that was crammed in the room which didn't leave much space for anything else. You can imagine how this caused a lot of frustration with many of us as we had no privacy, especially after you've been told off by your mum and your brothers and sisters are mocking you. There was nowhere to hide and sulk by yourself.

My mum was a very homely person but suffered with high blood pressure. By the time I was eight or nine years old, my mum officially stopped full-time working, so she was mostly at home when my dad was out. Looking back, I don't know how my mum coped with so many children. She would say, "It is the grace of God that keeps me going." Sometimes when things did get a bit heated, to get some order, she would un-leash, "Wait till your father gets home." Hearing that would just stop me in my tracks and then I would be nagging her to change her mind about telling my dad. In her Jamaican accent, she would say, "You're raising mi blood pressure, Mervin!"

On some occasions, my mum didn't change her mind and you knew you were in big trouble. I would go upstairs to the bedroom and just hope my dad didn't call me when he got in. He would stand at the bottom of the stairs, and I will never forget the distinctive way he used to call my name with his deep Jamaican accent. It was a long 'Mer' and short 'vin' - 'Merrrrrrr-vin' - and he didn't have to say come downstairs, you just knew you had to go.

What was so funny—well, not so funny at the time—was that when he started telling you off or handing out one of his creative punishments like: clean all the doors, wipe all the skirting boards down, clean the dog poo in the back garden, clean up the front garden and next door's too - was that my mum would be telling my dad to calm down,'Okay G, Okay G.'

G was short for Gladstone, my dad's name. So, Mum would snitch on me and then try and stop Dad for what was coming next—which was a bit annoying to be fair. I'm not knocking her because she was the best woman in the world, my greatest role model. However, Dad was the man when you wanted the sentence carried out and the punishments executed. I remember saying to myself that I never wanted to be that guy, getting called upon just to dish out punishments. Dad was good at it and, unconsciously, I was learning all of his sanction techniques. The three Ls were in full effect - **Life Long Learning** - I just didn't know at the time what impact it would have later on in my life.

Dad was in the Cato Hall of fame back in Portland, Jamaica for his disciplinary skills. When my younger brother went to Jamaica just before the lockdown, he met our older cousins who said their parents used to call Uncle G to come and discipline them. Bulroy, one of my cousins, said when my dad came back to Jamaica on holiday, he saw him at a family member's house. Bulroy was a smoker and my dad offered him a cigarette. Bulroy fell apart and nervously refused the cigarette. At the time, Bulroy was 40! That's how afraid he was of his Uncle G. Such was the reputation of my dad as a disciplinarian.

I mentioned earlier in this book that when my son was at secondary school, he was getting into a lot of trouble both at school and at home with his mum. By now, I had all of my dad's telling-off techniques stored in my memory bank and all the body language and facial expressions to go with them. When Wesley's mum would call me and ask me to speak to Wesley for being rude to her, I would warn him that if he didn't behave himself, I would confiscate his gadgets. When I said I was going to do something, I would definitely follow it through. When the calls came from his mother, there I was to hand out the discipline. I had a drawer full of Wesley's gadgets and Nintendo games. It got to the point when Wesley was finding excuses not to come to my house on weekends because he was really getting to dislike me. All I did was dish out punishments.

I was getting really good at verbally disciplining children to the point family members would call me to come to their house to tell off their kids and get them to do their chores. Their parents would even say to them, 'I'm going to tell Uncle Mervin to come and sort you out.' The news got around town that I was good at this thing and people from the church started asking me to tell off their children too. I remember my mum's friend called me and told me that one of her teenage daughters was playing up and she wanted me to talk to her. I visited the house and my mum's friend said, 'Mervin you might as well speak to both of my daughters because they are both playing up.' I look back on it now and cringe. I had become a Mini G.

I guess I thought if I could discipline Wesley then he would start behaving himself, keep his mum off my back and everything would be okay. Well, it didn't go that way and the calls from his

teachers started to ramp up and I had to start going to his school for meetings about his behaviour.

Around this time, Wesley was also playing up
big time at my house. This is when we decided to have our first family meeting when **STOP,
START, CONTINUE** was introduced. As I said
in the previous chapter, I got to learn so much
more about my son during this period but even
more about myself.

When I really spoke to Wesley, I realised this boy
felt that nothing was going his way. His mother
was in a steady relationship with a man who was
now living in his house, and to Wesley, he wasn't
ready for this change. He was not getting on with
his mother's partner and I think some of that was
down to Wesley. It was an unsettling time for him,
and he didn't even understand why his behaviour
was so erratic.

When I finally got the "light bulb" moment, I
felt so guilty. But I knew it had to be all about my
son, Wesley, and I just wanted to show him the
love that I had for him.

I spoke to Sophia, and we agreed that we wanted him to come and live with us, so I started to have talks with his mum about this as a possibility. I had discussions with the school I was working at about a possible transfer for Wesley and they gave me the green light.

I intentionally made the decision to go on a mission, to eradicate the method I was using to discipline children in the family. I had to start to cleanse it out of my system by communicating differently with Wesley first. When I got a call about his behaviour, I would have a discussion with Wesley and unpick the individual incident using the same techniques I would be using with the children at school. It worked for them, so why wouldn't it work with my family and friends' children? I was in a disciplinary old-fashioned culture bubble, a Mini G.

Well, that bubble was going to be burst because I didn't want another generation in my bloodline to continue it. No more was I going to be that guy telling off all the children I loved. I was determined to show them something different—the art of listening, communicating, the power of empathy and getting to the root of the problem. Many of our young people go through different types of traumas, and putting plasters over the wounds can just make things worse.

One Christmas, there was a family event and some of my younger nephews and nieces were giving some lip to my daughters and some of their older cousins. When we got home that night, our daughters were complaining about their behaviour and how the older cousins were saying if it were back in the old days, Uncle Mervin would have sorted them out, but now he was a soft touch. To be honest, I can live with that.

It looks as if I have broken that old disciplinary chain as Wesley has a lovely relationship with his sons. He is firm but fair and is always explaining things to them. I think I can safely say, mission accomplished.

LEARNING

Discipline - It starts with you (the parent). Don't give away your parenting role. Here are some questions for you to consider:

- When you think about discipline, what immediately comes to mind?

- Do you discipline your children today the same way your parents disciplined you growing up?

- Are you listening to understand your children or are you listening to respond?

- What memories do you have of the way you were disciplined by your parents?

- How do past relationships impact the way you parent your children?

- On reflection, how could you be more effective in the discipline of your children going forward into the future?

- Do you think you are child-centred or parent-centred in your approach to the disciplining of your children?

- Do you discipline from a perspective that makes your life easier, or factors in your child's self-esteem and personal growth?

- Having reflected on the questions above, have you taken the time to examine the way in which you have used discipline in the past?

I recommend parents to go on a "Strengthening Families, Strengthening Communities" programme as this will help with all the questions above and more.

Chapter Three

Back to School Again

In the year 2000, the schools in London start-ed experiencing a different type of behaviour coming in from our streets. The rise of gang cul-ture was having a major effect on students in ed-ucation. Whether you were in a gang or not, the knock-on effect in the schools was impactful and teachers needed more support.

Learning mentoring was a new initiative that came from the United States (USA) with so many positive reports about how mentors were chang-ing the lives of the hard-to-reach kids on the streets in USA schools that it became a new tool for our schools.

The Labour government (at the time) decided to plough extra funding into education to bring learning mentoring into the schools and a massive recruitment programme kicked off.

By now, my life had turned around and a few people said they thought I'd be a good mentor. My thoughts were that over years, I (with a few associates) had spent so long messing up the community that now it was a chance for me to try and redeem myself. It was time for a little payback.

So, I took a leap of faith having no experience and asked my sister, Marlene, to write an application for me for the position of a learning mentor in a local Edmonton secondary school.

Marlene has always been great at writing applications and she was able to write some really good things about my past, even stuff I didn't remember. She got me through to the interview stage and I remember turning up that morning to the school for the interview process full of hope. That was soon put on pause when I saw there were another 11 people applying for just two mentoring posts. The school made all the candidates turn up at the same time and had us sit in the staff room eyeing up the competition.

Being back in a school setting in a staff room felt very surreal to me, and not in a good way. The only experience I'd had with school staff rooms was when I was at school and my teachers would ask the good kids to go fetch a senior member of staff from the staff room to come and remove me from their classroom, and that happened quite a few times. I disliked my time at school; however, I won't lie, I also had loads of fun, but that will be revealed some other time - maybe in the next book!

Most of the candidates there that morning were already from an educational background, and they started having conversations around the table using all this school educational jargon that I didn't understand, so I just kept quiet. I was actually thinking, 'What am I doing here? There is no way I'm going to get this job and I hate being in this school environment anyway. It's bringing all the bad memories back.' I just sat there in a daze like a fish out of water.

It was a long day. We had to complete a self-evaluation survey and write a report about a case study they had given us, which I didn't have a clue about. Then, finally, an interview with the Head of Inclusion, Deputy Head *and* the Head of the in-school Behaviour Unit. When I walked into that room, it felt like I was back in the 80s on one of those terrible parent evening nights when all the teachers would tell my dad how bad I'd been in every lesson apart from P.E. (nearly all the black kids at my school seemed to excel in Physical Education). My first thought was that the only person missing in that room was my dad.

To be honest, I don't remember what I said in the interview to this day as it was all a nervous blur. That evening, I got a call from the Head of the Behaviour Unit saying, 'We had two posts available, but we decided to recruit three candidates and we are happy to say you are one of them. Will you accept the post?' I replied 'Yes, of course' but in my head, I said, 'Wow, there is truly a God, God is real,' as I honestly believed I could have only gotten that job through God. One could argue I was just the right type of person they were looking for, but if you'd actually seen the other candidates –

you'd probably reconsider that argument because looking at those other applicants and then looking at me – I really didn't reflect the ideal person for the job.

A few weeks later, September 2001, I started the mentoring and one of the first students I had was a 13-year-old boy who I will call Jake. So, Jake was referred to me for constant disruptive behaviour in class, being disrespectful to most teachers, truanting lessons, lateness to school, lateness to lessons, wearing incorrect uniform, never making an attempt to complete homework, not bringing the correct equipment to school, going around with the wrong crowd, getting into fights, and so on and so on. Because of this, he was at risk of being permanently excluded. Having a mentor was going to be his last chance.

At first, Jake was very apprehensive about opening up to me, but to cut a long story short, it transpired that Jake's parents separated eight months before I started working with him. Jake was living with his dad at the weekends in a different part of London, pretty far away, which was one of the reasons why he was always very late on Monday mornings and tired most of the time throughout the week. His dad allowed him to do whatever he wanted over the weekend, which usually meant him coming home in the early hours of the morning. More distressingly was the relationship between his mum and dad, which was toxic, and without going into more detail, it was the whole reason why this young man's life was falling apart.

It was a tough slog trying to keep this young man in school as most of his teachers didn't want him there and complained to the head teacher several times about him. I had to try and get him to reinvent himself, which was working to a certain extent, but it was often two steps forward and one step back. I knew the only way of rescuing Jake from permanent exclusion and stopping him from ending up in the pupil referral unit (PRU) was to engage with his parents.

I started having short weekly telephone conversations with them individually about his progress and just getting to know them on a different level, building up a professional but positive relationship with them both. Then after a few months had passed I thought it was time to speak to both parents together. I was very nervous about the prospect of this, but I knew it had to be done. I set the meeting date, the time and the venue – which was to be in the school. How I wish Zoom had been around back then.

We met and I put some rules in place like no talking over each other, etc. I look back on it now and think how bold I was to take such a risk as I was new to this mentoring thing. However, I also remembered that I'd had mates who had been permanently excluded and I'd seen where most of them ended up. I didn't want this for Jake.

The meeting started really frosty and could have gone left on a few occasions. I won't go into detail about the meeting but I'll just say we were able to all agree on some simple but effective targets, which were reviewed regularly.

This meeting was a game-changer in the life of Jake. He struggled at first with some of the boundaries we put in place, but it worked out for him in the end He didn't get excluded and I didn't need to work with him any longer because after four months of having that meeting, he was doing so well. Yes, he had bumps in the road after that, no one can change overnight, but the door was always open for him to touch base with me, which he did on several occasions.

I learned so much through this experience, but I must share something else I learned with you - Jake was actually a clever kid. In some of our sessions, we were able to complete some homework as he knew it wasn't going to happen at his dad's house. In these sessions, Jake literally taught me how to use Microsoft Word. I used to have to send emails and didn't know what I was doing, I didn't even know how to get rid of all these squiggly red lines under words... well, he taught me all about sorting out spelling mistakes and so many other things about Microsoft Word. It was truly back to school again for me. Life Long Learning from a child on the verge of permanent exclusion. I was teaching him, but he was also teaching me. I was able to complete my end-of-term reports on a computer with no problem, which was something that I had been really worried about.

There is so much more I could say in this chapter about what children go through when parents separate—I've been through it as a parent myself. I know it is so important to put the child first and try your hardest to put your grievances about each other aside to make sure your child (children) feel as stable as possible which I know from personal experience is easier said than done.

LEARNING

Here are some questions for you to consider:

- Can you prioritize clear and consistent communication about your child's needs, even if you disagree?

- Are you willing to put your child's well-being above your own conflicts?

- How can you create a communication plan to minimize confusion for your child?

- Are you open to discussing and potentially modifying the parenting plan as your child's needs evolve?

- How might your child be feeling about the separation?

- What are your child's individual needs and how can you best support them emotionally?

- Is your child struggling with any practical aspects of the new living situation?

- How can you encourage your child to openly communicate their feelings and concerns?

- Can you maintain some consistency in routines and expectations between your households?

- How can you ensure clear and consistent discipline across both homes?

- Are there important traditions or events you can continue to celebrate together as a family?

- How can you help your child feel secure and loved despite the changes?

- Would it be beneficial to seek professional guidance on co-parenting or communication strategies?

- Are there support groups or resources available for children of separated parents?

- Do you have a trusted network of friends and family who can support you and your child?

By reflecting on these questions, parents can develop a more collaborative approach to co-parenting during a separation, prioritizing the child's well-being and emotional security.

Also, if you have someone you both trust, please allow them to mediate if they are up for it.

And remember Microsoft Word - Our children can teach us as well!

Chapter Four

All Blacks

If you type "Top 10 Greatest Sports Teams of All Time" into Google, guess what team comes up as number one? Not the Brazilian football team of the 70s or the West Indies cricket team of the 80s, but it's the All Blacks Rugby Team of the 90s.

I wouldn't call myself a rugby fan, but I do watch it when they have the big international tournaments. The only individual name that sticks out to me is Jonah Lomu who played for the New Zealand All Blacks. Lomu destroyed England in the 1995 Rugby World Cup. He absolutely flattened Mike Catt before scoring one of his most-watched tries on YouTube. But as an International team, the name of the All Blacks stands out as one of the most famous sporting teams ever.

I remember a few years ago, some of my family members, mainly my brothers and older nephews, decided to take all the younger boys in the family out for a meal and a chat. There were quite a few of us who went that day. We invited one of our close family friends, Justin Cochrane, to also come with us and chat to the boys. Justin at the time was the Youth Team coach at Tottenham Hotspurs football club. The boys' ages ranged between 10 to 18 and a few of the older crew were there in attendance like me. The meal went down well. Good food can often be a catalyst for good conversation.

As coach of a football team, Justin was keen to get into the subject matter of teamwork, which started with him asking the boys the question, 'Name the teams you admire the most?' They all gave the most obvious answers and mentioned all the most popular football teams—Arsenal, Arsenal and more Arsenal! (I'm only joking... as you can guess, I'm an Arsenal fan) In any case, I'm also a general lover of football and so is Justin,

so whilst mostly football teams were mentioned –
Liverpool, Chelsea, Manchester City - Justin was
actually heading in another sporting direction.

Justin said, 'All the teams you've mentioned are
good teams, but the question was, name the team
you most admire?" The team I admire the most is
the New Zealand All Blacks rugby team.'

Justin pointed out all the reasons why he loved
this rugby team, but what was evident was that it
wasn't all about their successes on the rugby pitch
which were numerous—winning 77% of their test
matches since 1903, winning the Rugby World
Cup three times and having been crowned Rugby
Championship winners 16 times. Justin was more
intrigued with their team culture and what made
it so strong - the substance that goes further than
physical fitness or team strategy or even rugby
pitch tactics. It was the ethos that was built on
humility, unity, and a deep reverence for the black
jersey with the silver fern.

For me, the All Blacks stand out more than any
other sporting team in the world and never more
so than when performing the Haka in front of

their opponents - a warrior dance - and all their opponents can do is watch, admire, and try not to be intimidated.

My Life Long Learning antenna was fully switched on and I was probably getting more out of this talk than anyone else as I was thinking about how I could incorporate some of All Blacks ethos into my own family.

It was a great night and made me want to do more in depth research and find out more about the history of the All Blacks. I learned that they embody the Māori concept of "whānau" which translates to FAMILY. Their strength as a team stems from this deep-seated cultural value that extends beyond the rugby pitch. A signature aspect of their solidarity is the Haka performed before each rugby match. It serves as a powerful symbol of their unity and a collective channelling of their energy and intentions. Their ethos, encompassing excellence, respect, and humility, is indoctrinated in every player that wears that black jersey. This ethos is not only a guiding principle but also a binding force, creating an environment where each member is committed to the success of the whole.

When I read this, I said in my head, 'Justin, you are Justin-credible! Wow, awesome that you mentioned this concept.' (Did you notice my play on words there? Just incredible with Justin-credible? Lol)

The Haka concept meant family and of course, how could it not mean that? It made perfect sense. They have a sense of unity unlike any other team I have ever seen. The Haka is powerful and gives you the idea that each player is so close with each other on and off the pitch, that they look like they would die for each other. The research said the members are committed to the success of everyone in the team. I thought "Wow" again, because to me, that is what family is meant to be.

This made me reflect on the culture and ethos of my own family. The substance and foundation, which forms our reputation. What do we do as a family that makes us who we are?

Our immediate family's Haka or secret weapon is prayer. We pray every Wednesday without fail at

8.15 p.m. Those who are not able to be physically present, tune in online. We have been doing this for years. I can't really tell you when we started but it's now a part of our DNA. I am a firm believer in families that pray together stay together. Our faith underpins everything we believe in. We even invite other family members and close friends to join us.

I always listen carefully to what people say about my immediate family, whether it's in jest or serious because, ultimately, what people see governs what they say. If different people say the same thing about your family, then whatever they say, that reputation will stick. I have heard many people say and joke that we as a family are always together. At first, when I kept on hearing it, I didn't think we were, but on reflection—and by the way, reflecting about your family culture is a good thing to do—I didn't realise just how often we went out together as a family. We get comments when we are all seen in the supermarket together by family and friends. Some people jokingly think we have brainwashed our children because we are together so much, but trust me, they have their own minds!

We celebrate together. If one wins, we all win. When one of our children got good school reports or test results, the whole family would celebrate together and make it clear that we have all done well because we are a team. Remember what the research said about the All Blacks—members are committed to the success of *everyone* in the team.

Recently, my grandson had his first parents' evening, and the teacher said some really lovely things about him. He is a good boy. We made sure the whole family expressed their delight and those who couldn't see him on the day made contact in other ways to celebrate with him. These things are important.

Our children always used to complain that we were always the first people to arrive at family events or any other appointments, engagements, etc. Showing your children the importance of getting to places on time - or in our case before time - starts with us as parents. These types of habits are passed down from generation to generation. Unfortunately, in some families, being late is a part of their culture, and for the sake of our children,

I was always determined that our offspring would grow up being on time.

Always helping people is another habit we as a family have formed. If I'm being honest, this has come from my wife. She is forever helping people. If we go out to a party or function, my wife ends up helping in the kitchen or helping to tidy and clear up—one for all and all for one. People like inviting us to functions because we come as a team and we all help together.

As a family, we set goals every year. Every January, we review our yearly individual goals and targets then set new ones. This gives us focus and direction about what we want to achieve for the year (See Chapter 12 -Words Are Powerful).

These are just a few components that make up our family's culture and ethos. We are a team, and like it or not, we have a reputation like most teams.

LEARNING

Here are some questions for you to consider:

- What are some stories or events that have

shaped your family's values?

- Are there any family mottos or sayings that resonate with your family?

- What do you hope to pass down to future generations?

- How do you want to be remembered as a family?

- What are the most important things in life for your family?

- How do you define success as a family?

- How important is individual expression compared to family unity?

- Does forgiveness come easily in your family? If not, why?

- Are there any important rituals or traditions you hold dear?

- What is your family's attitude towards

money and possessions?

Chapter Five

The Rites of Passage

Let me introduce you to Zandile Mthethwa from South Africa. She was a member of the church my family and I attended, and had two sons - Musa, 11 and Tshepo, 13. I had known her boys for a few years as I had been their Sunday school teacher. As a single mum, Zandile worked hard to give those boys all she could. She had no family in the U.K apart from a cousin in Manchester. Most of her family were in South Africa, as was the father of the boys.

The unusual thing was that Zandile was Jewish. She attended both a Pentecostal church and her local Synagogue, so she kind of had two families and two communities supporting her and the boys. I look back now and really admire the way she looked after those two boys.

I remember attending Zandile's oldest boy Tshepo's Bar Mitzvah. That was a real eye-opener for me. If you have never been to one before, it's a celebration for young Jewish boys and girls when they reach the age of 13. It's like bringing them into adulthood.

I remember Tshepo training to read Hebrew scriptures, some that had to be memorised and some from the scrolls they had. This training lasted for 12 months. I just couldn't believe that at the age of 13, he could remember so much and then, at the end of the service, he gave a fantastic speech. I thought, 'Wow, he is truly a man now.' I also remember looking at Zandile and seeing that she must have felt like the proudest mother in the world.

The service was packed with representatives of both faith communities. One half of the congregation were black African and Caribbean Pentecostal loud Christians, and the other half were white quiet Jewish people – as different as chalk &

cheese. But it worked. All of us from church were so happy to have been invited. I said to my wife Sophia that we should be doing this in our family, for our children. Our normal birthday parties are music, food, cutting the cake, line dancing to Candy (a song by the pop group Cameo) and then more dancing, food and cake!

After the service, the celebration continued in the adjacent hall with food, presents and speeches. Wow! I wish I had had something like this when I was 13. I think it would have given me more accountability, purpose and responsibility and may have even kept me out of trouble.

After attending this event, I was determined to incorporate something like this for my family, but I knew this would be a massive mind set and culture change and no one person could do it.

I come from a very, **very** big family as my father had 18 children, 11 with my mother and all of the 11 now had their own children and some of them were now grandparents like me. So how was I going to get this concept out to all of them and bring everyone on this exciting journey with me?

I am a member of a few groups that do various family or community work. Above The Clouds is a family group that consists of my two younger brothers, Lloyd and Bobby, and my two nephews, Corey and Aaron. In one of our weekly meetings, I mentioned what I witnessed at the Bar Mitzvah, and I also discussed the benefits to the young people, and the whole family.

We decided we wanted to set up a steering group, which would consist of at least one person from each of the 11 families.

You may not have a large family like mine to do something like this, but the good thing is you don't need to. This can also be done with friends, your faith groups or even with people from your community.

We wanted to make sure the steering group would be made up of all age groups so we would get a wide range of ideas and a communication link that would reach out to all members of our family.

We got the group together and decided to call it The Rites of Passage. We had our first meeting face to face just before the Covid lockdown kicked in, and then that was a whole new ball game as everything went online. We started to have weekly online meetings and, to be honest, after the first few weeks of technical issues, we got it sorted. The meetings were productive and I actually think we were able to make more ground because of the lockdown.

Not only were we able to arrange a future celebration event for our young people who reached the age of 13, but we also had a full package of what we thought our young people should have in place. We named it C.R.O.P : Cato Rites of Passage.

We believed that all our young people should have a foundation in place to give them a "leg up" or advantage, before they are officially classed as adults. Similar to what other cultures or families do, we wanted to make it intentional.

The Rites of Passage steering group arranged our first version of a Bar Mitzvah, which we decided to call the C.R.O.P Harvest Celebration. It was for my nephew, Xavier, who was turning 13.

Straight after the end of Lockdown, he was going to be the first Cato to have this celebration.

We obviously made a few adjustments from the Jewish traditional celebration since we do originate from Jamaica, so we felt we had to make it "our own".

The hall was decorated in the theme of Jamaica using green, yellow and black, with music playing in the background. The Rites of Passage steering group was all uniformed in white T-shirts with the C.R.O.P logo that we designed printed on the right of our chests. We had rum punch & non-alcoholic punch waiting for our guests when they arrived.

C.R.O.P Logo

We started with food. You must feed our people first if you really want us to be in a good mood!

When everyone was full, then the real ceremony began with a prayer. Leading up to this event, Xavier had to read Psalms 91, which was Xavier's late great-grandmother's favourite scripture. He also had to learn, memorise and recite the famous Psalms 23. After a few speeches from his grandparents, mum, and then his dad, there were a few party games. Xavier gave his speech and then was taken around the back and given his C.R.O.P T-shirt, which he put on and came back out to rapturous applause.

Xavier was now officially a young adult—the first Cato to have this special ceremony - this new family ritual that was going to change the whole way our family commemorated such things going forward. Then finally, the last part of the ceremony – a floating helium balloon with a string was stuck to the table and everyone started sticking £5, £10, and £20 pound notes to the balloon using Blutac. The balloon was soon totally covered, so everyone then started sticking the money onto the actual balloon string! Xavier said this was definitely his favourite part of the event!

There are a few things that have been really special in our Cato's history like when my mother won the Mother of the Year award or when my sister, Lurine, won a Queen's honour, an MBE and maybe a few other things, but this was right up there with them. A very special occasion and many say a turning point in our family's culture.

My niece, Ava, is next in line to turn 13 and have her C.R.O.P Harvest Celebration. She is so excited and can't wait for her turn. And we can't wait to celebrate her turn too.

LEARNING

What would be in your family's Rites of Passage? See below our Cato Rights of Passage. Hopefully they will give you some ideas when creating your own.

Ages 0-5

- 1st Birthday Celebration Support (Helping Out/Ideas)

- Passport Advice

- Bank Account Advice

- Blessing of the Child Support/Advice

- Christmas Graduation support

Ages 6-11

(Workshops can be taught by people outside the family if you wish not to lead on these workshops.)

- Workshop – Basic Money Management

- Workshop – Basic Sex Education

- Workshop – Black History

- Advice about Swimming lessons

Ages 12-16

- C.R.O.P style Harvest Becoming of Age Celebration (13)/Helping Organising

- Workshop – Advanced Sex Education Workshop

- Workshop – Advanced Black History

- Exam Support

- Careers/Apprenticeships Advice, Etc.

Ages 17-18

- Driving Lesson Info/Advice

- Careers/Apprenticeships Advice, Etc.

- Create Vision Board Support

Chapter Six

F1 Experience

S adly, the story about Zandile did not finish on a note of celebration. Let me share some more.

About five months after Tshepo's Bar Mitzvah, it was a normal Saturday morning for me with my Christian men's group in Jubilee Park where we trained and prayed every Saturday morning without fail. In the middle of prayer, my mobile phone started ringing. I was upset with myself because I normally remember to put it on silent when we start praying. I wasn't going to answer but it kept on ringing, and when I looked on the screen, I saw it was Florence—a member of the church we attended. I was surprised that she would be calling me so early on a Saturday morning.

I answered, 'Florence, is everything OK?'

She replied, 'Mervin, Zandile has passed away.'

I said, 'What?' in confusion.

She responded, 'Yes, Zandile passed away, she had a cardiac arrest this morning at home.'

I was stunned. I could not believe what Florence was saying. I had seen Zandile in church the week before and she had seemed fine.

This sad news shocked me, but my immediate thought and next question was, 'What about the boys?'

Florence said, 'The Rabbi of the Synagogue is with them now at the hospital.'

I immediately called Zandile's house number. A man picked up the phone and I identified myself as a friend of Zandile who attended her church. The voice at the other end of the phone introduced himself as Colin, the Rabbi from her synagogue. He told me that Zandile passed away that morning and she had made him, Colin, her next of kin six weeks ago without even telling him, and he was now responsible for the boys.

All of a sudden, a flood of questions rushed through my mind. Next of kin? Only six weeks ago? Did she know she didn't have much time? Why the Rabbi? Why not someone from her church? Why not her cousin in Manchester? What was she thinking?

If I'm really honest, I don't even remember how we finished the conversation as my head was fuzzy with confusion and a range of different emotions.

In the years since, I realised how right Zandile was with the decisions she made. She was truly a woman of wisdom, always thinking about what was best for her boys.

A couple of days after the sad news, a few members of the church were selected to meet Rabbi Colin Eimer and his wife, Dee. I was part of the team. I really didn't know what to expect but my wife and I already decided whatever the Eimers' and the children needed, we would support them.

We met outside the Eimers' house, and it was decided by the lead pastor that we would allow them to say what they wanted. When we entered the house, we saw the boys and they looked sad but well. The Eimers' explained that they would look after the boys and take care of everything. I had already decided that I would have a separate conversation with them after this meeting, which I did.

My wife, Sophia, and I had a discussion about the meeting, and we were both still in agreement that we wanted to support the Eimers and the boys in any way we could. So, I rang the Rabbi and asked if they could keep our family in the picture with whatever was happening concerning the boys—not much was said but just a soft thank you from Dee, the Rabbi's wife.

A week later, we got a call from the Eimers inviting us to their house to have a chat about the boys.

We accepted the invitation, and the following week, went to their house with our two daughters, Helena and Hannah, who were younger than the boys but knew them well from Sunday school.

When we arrived, we met Musa and Tshepo in the passageway. They seemed happier and more settled than the last time I saw them. We were then taken to the back room, which had a revolving table with a selection of bowls of food.

It was definitely the chat around a revolving round table that I will never forget. It started with normal standard chit-chat with some lovely nibbles being spun to each person as the table revolved. It was a time of just softly getting to know each other. As mentioned before, food makes a lot of difference when you are having a discussion with people, especially if you don't really know them.

Musa, Tshepo and the girls went to the front room to play PlayStation, and this gave the Eimers the chance to have a deeper discussion with us about the boys.

Dee, the Rabbi's wife was well-versed and comfortable with a conversation like this as she had worked supporting families in the community for over 30 years. She got straight to the point, 'Colin and I are on the brink of retirement, we are obviously not the same colour as the boys and we are asking for your support.'

We knew exactly want she meant. Yes, they may have been from the same religion, but culturally, there were obvious differences and also the age gap between the Eimers and the boys was at least 60 years. By now, the Eimers were aware that I worked for the local council in education, and that my wife was a teacher. I am sure they may even have spoken to the boys about our family to get some kind of character reference. They probably wanted to make sure they weren't entertaining mass murderers! But in the midst of all this turmoil for the boys and the dramatic change of circumstances for the Eimers, it was reassuring to know that our support was needed in this unfortunate situation.

Usually in my day job, my favourite response to questions of support is, 'What does this support look like?' Well, in this circumstance, the question went out the window as the answer was obvious. My wife and I looked at each other and said, 'Of course we will support you.'

What was evident in the following year was some of the challenges the Eimers and the boys faced.

The fight with social services was a massive challenge as news broke out that they wanted to send the boys to South Africa to live with their grandmother. Financially, that would be much cheaper for social services, but the boys were British. They didn't know South Africa, and the area they would be living in was still unsettled when it came to violence. After a long battle with social services and support from friends, the boys were able to stay with the Eimers as they had become their legal guardians and were able to get them into a good community Jewish school.

The boys were also going through trauma and falling out with each other, which led to physical fights, and on a couple of occasions, I had to go and have a word with them. Not as Mini G but as the "new me". Other challenges this new family had to face were more fundamental - getting to know each other and settling into these new family dynamics. To assist Colin and Dee, they pulled in their community around the boys to support them financially, emotionally, educationally, socially, recreationally – there wasn't a stone left unturned.

I've always been a great fan of Formula 1 racing and this increased when Lewis Hamilton signed for Mercedes. The part I love the most is when Lewis has been racing for 20 or so laps and he pulls up in a pitstop. His team have less than eight seconds to stop the car, gather around it, jack it up, take off the old tires and replace them with new ones, make some repairs, a few mechanical adjustments, clean off his visor and then he is off again with the car looking like it did at the start of the race – brand-new. You see teamwork like never before with every one of the members of his pitstop crew all knowing exactly what role they play and how to execute it.

Lewis Hamilton has won seven world championships with Mercedes and is clearly the face of Mercedes, but for me, the person who makes everything work is Toto Wolfe, the team principal and chief executive of Mercedes F1. He is the one who pulls team Mercedes together and makes it work the way it works. When Lewis wins, the whole construction team wins too.

Well, what I'm trying to say is Musa and Tshepo are like the Lewis Hamilton of this world - they are living and running their race, lap after lap. They are the "new" face of the family and we all want them to succeed. Dee and Colin Eimer are like Toto Wolfe. They ultimately have made sure that the boys have had the right people around them, supporting them, knowing the jobs they have to execute whether things go right or wrong and the boys are in the pitstop getting that support. When the boys win, we all win and celebrate together... that is Haka, that is teamwork, that is F1 – Family 1st.

If you had to choose one chapter out of this book to read again, I would want it to be this one. Why is it so important? Because so many of our children do not have a support network built around them. We know there are so many single-parent families out there like Zandile and her boys, but she was able to wrap two different communities around her children and put something in place just in case something happened to her. That's what Toto Wolfe's do – they plan around their "children" and are forward thinkers.

If you are reading this book and are a parent or carer, I can't emphasise enough how important it is that you have a team or crew around your children and you don't call on them only when things go wrong. You are Toto Wolfe... it's your job to make the people supporting your child feel like part of the team. If you have family members you have fallen out with but they are good for your child, you should put your feelings aside so that the relationship with them and your child still stays strong. Far too many times, family members or parents break up and the child loses members of their support network.

Musa and Tshepo have grown up into lovely young men and I spoke to them to get permission to include their story in this book. Tshepo told me that he and his brother are so grateful for the continuous support they have received from everyone. In some cultures, this wrap-around support is standard. In others, there is a little bit more work to be done but it all starts with one Toto Wolfe.

LEARNING

Here are some questions for you to consider:

- What are the most important values you hope your child will develop?

- Can you describe some qualities you admire in people who interact with your child?

- How would you like someone to handle a situation where your child is struggling or making a mistake?

- What kind of support system do you envision for your child outside of the immediate family? (E.g. mentors, coaches, teachers.)

- How important is it for the people who support your child to share similar interests or hobbies?

- When it comes to your child's activities

(sports, clubs, etc.), what qualities are you looking for in a coach or leader?

- How would you like to be kept informed about your child's progress and development? (E.g. regular updates, open communication.)

- How important is it for you to collaborate with the people who support your child in making decisions?

- Is there anything specific about your child's personality or learning style that you think would be helpful for someone who supports them to know?

- Are there any activities or interests you'd particularly like someone to encourage or support in your child?

- Is there anything you'd like the people who support your child to avoid doing or saying?

Chapter Seven

Let's Make a Perfect Parent

If you had to make a perfect parent cake, what ingredients would you need?

OK, let me ask this a little differently - what qualities do you think the perfect parent should have?

Just after the lockdown, I hosted a few parenting podcast shows. One of the shows was called Let's Make a Perfect Parent. I had a three-way discussion with Ayse Adil, CEO of a family mediation company called Family Based Solutions, and Laverne Antrobus, a child psychologist and TV presenter. We set ourselves the task of making a perfect parent cake by agreeing on what ingredients needed to be included for the perfect bake.

It's not surprising that listening skills was the first quality mentioned. If you remember in one of the previous chapters - Changing of a Culture - I had to learn the hard way. If you are a busy parent like me and your life is nonstop, you should try and find time to listen to your children. On the podcast, Ayse mentioned opportune times to speak to your children like on the way to school and coming back from school. Ayse explained how parents could start conversations by using open questions like, 'What was really good about your day today?' Isn't that better than the normal, 'How was school today?' Most of the time, you get the same answer, 'Fine,' and that's the end of that conversation.

For some reason, listening to our children can be difficult, especially when they only have something to say when you are at your busiest. BUT, you really should try and make time and really hear what they are saying.

The following week on the podcast, the topic was Quality Time - The Truth. It was another three-way conversation, but this time with two of my closest friends, Karen Allen, author and single-parent of five children, and Robert George, a family worker and parenting guru. The theme was having quality time with your family. I hosted the show but I could not concentrate. I kept on getting flashbacks of my daughter when she was younger shouting out, 'Family Time!'

The phrase 'Family Time' will go down in folk-lore within my household.

A few years after we started our family meetings and the **STOP, START, CONTINUE** mechanism was well-oiled, my youngest daughter, Helena, gave the whole family a '**START**' on her **STOP, START, CONTINUE** sheet. It was to start having family time. This was a time in my life where it was just work, work and more work. Yes, I was a workaholic and I can honestly say I was hardly, if at all, giving my family any quality time and that was definitely the truth. I've always had a good work ethic, but when you have a good work ethic *and* you love your job *and* you have a family... well, let's just say if you don't find balance, you're in trouble.

Helena was aged around six or seven at the time and I'm not sure what TV programme she watched to give her another idea to stop me in my tracks again but I'm sure she must have been watching a Peppa Pig episode because it didn't sound like she got the idea from Dora the Explorer! Maybe she'd had enough of being overlooked and wanted some real quality time with her family. It was her **START** request, and just like that, she hit me with another knockout blow. This time, it was a message for everyone, and I had to admit that boy, was Helena right.

What I loved about the **STOP, START, CONTINUE** tool was that every time I cast it to one side, it would come back and smack me right in the face. It was time again for me to listen to my daughter and so we introduced 'Family Time'.

I have some great memories of my family during 'Family Time'. This was where listening came back into play as we asked our children what they wanted to do. Yes, it can seem like a risky question, but our children didn't ask for much and I think I enjoyed it more than they did. We played games like Hide and Seek in the dark - what a classic! The screams and the laughter we shared are unforgettable. However, one of my favourites was Indoor non-stop cricket with a bat and ball made out of tonnes of paper and Sellotape (a brand name for sticky tape). We played it in the passage, and trust me, I was never going to let them beat me. Anyone who knows me knows I can be very competitive. Don't let the kids win all the time, let them work hard for those wins. You can actually teach them a lot during play too.

Helena took 'Family Time' to another level. Sophia and I would be having a debate about nothing and Helena would just jump in the middle of us, star-shaped, and shout out, 'Family Time!' and that would be the trigger to kick off the fun and games. When she saw me working for too long on the laptop, she would say, 'Come on, dad... Family Time!' I started buying the games my mother used to play with me and my brothers and sisters—Playing cards, Frustration, Connect Four and Draughts.

Dominos became a very competitive game in my house and my daughters got so good that they started to "read" the game, which basically meant they could tell what domino pieces people had in their hands. We all got really good to the point when visitors came to the house, the girls were desperate to get at them with a game, especially the older West Indian male friends of mine who always claimed to be great at dominos, like my friend Rudolph Walker. We always said no guest can come to our home and beat us at any game, and boy did Rudolph get a thrashing that day. That is another story that has gone down in our family folklore.

In order to have regular fun with your family, you have to make quality family time for them. Maybe you can agree a slot with your family once a week to start off, but more importantly be intentional, plan it and be consistent. You could even get your immediate family, uncles, aunts, cousins, friends - to all join in.

Having fun was one of the qualities mentioned in the podcast – so have fun and add an ingredient to your 'perfect parent' cake.

LEARNING

Parenting Self-Assessment

Where do you think you are? Feel free to add/amend qualities. You can mark yourself or be brave and ask your child to mark you and discuss how you can go up a mark. Go back to this in a months' time to see what has changed.

Qualities	Marks out of 10 1 - Need a bit of work. 10 - Perfect.
Affectionate	
Empathy	
Good Listener	
Having Fun	
Teaching Independence	
Having quality time	
Communication	
Being Kind	
Managing boundaries	

Chapter Eight

Attention, Attention

You would be surprised how some family members can get your attention by doing the wrong thing. Young people crave attention, that 'Look at me!' syndrome. And if they cannot get good attention, then bad will have to do.

I will never forget when I was young, maybe 13 or 14 years old, that my dad never came to watch me play football. I was a pretty good footballer even in primary school. A lot of the other parents turned up to watch a game, particularly my friends who were white. I remember going to games and always having to go in my friend's dad's car. I felt hurt.

By the time I got to secondary school, the situation had not changed, but this particular time,

I don't know why, I really wanted someone from my family to turn up and watch me play. So, I lied. I told my dad and my brother that I was scoring five goals every game. I kept lying, coming in after every game and saying I scored another five goals just to get somebody to come and watch me play football.

And then came the game I will never forget—although it was many years ago, it is etched in my memory. I played against Winchmore School for my school, Aylward, and I was playing on the wing. I saw my dad watching me from the street through the school railings. When I saw him, I thought, 'Right, I am not going to pass this ball, I am just going to be the greediest player ever. I have got my daddy watching me.' I was so greedy when I received the ball, I would just take on all the players and go for the goal. All because my dad was watching me. I can still remember how I felt—I was scared I would not live up to his expectations. During the game, my teammates called me greedy, but by the end, they were congratulating me on how well I had played, and I managed to score five goals!

I cannot remember if my dad said anything to me afterwards, but his very presence made me give it my all. It just goes to show what can happen when the right person is there watching you, especially your dad who you always want to please.

What this experience taught me as a parent was to be there for whatever my kids did if I possibly could. Sports events, parents' evenings, meetings in school, option choices, etc. By turning up, you are showing your children this is as important to you as it is to them. As a dad, I made this my priority whether the news was going to be good, or bad.

A friend of mine, Robert George, is a parenting guru. He runs a 'Caring Dads' group where he discusses 'child-centred parenting' and 'adult-centred parenting'. The difference is that adult-centred parenting is when the child is participating on your journey and child-centred parenting is when you as a parent are with your child on their journey.

An example from my own life is when I had my son, Wesley, at weekends. He would do everything with me, but it was nearly all what I wanted to do. He would come with me to do shopping, he would meet my friends, and he would visit my brothers. It was all about me. It was my agenda and he had to follow it. Yes, and I was one of those McDonald's dads who took him there for food as that was what I thought he would like. If he had a Happy Meal, I had done my job! Occasionally, I would arrange for him to meet with his cousins of the same age but that didn't require much effort from me. In the evenings, he would be dropped at my mum's where he would sleep, and I would go out about my business and see him in the morning. That is a perfect example of adult-centred parenting.

By the time I had my two daughters and I was in a stable relationship, I was in a different place and I had learnt differently. What I was now able to do was exhibit more child-centred parenting. My younger daughter still reminds me about when I went to daddy and daughters' art club. Now, those who know me know being artistic is not how I would describe myself. But I signed up anyway and we went along to the local library and started drawing together. My daughter was in her element and I was enjoying it as well.

We went every week, and it became a very important bonding time for us both. My daughter was only five at the time but these sessions spurred her on and she is now in sixth form doing A Level Art and will be using these skills in her future career. Unsurprisingly, I am not sure it did much for my artistic talents!

My learning from this is that my daughter doesn't remember all the presents I have bought her over the years, she doesn't remember all the trips to McDonald's but this experience and those like it are what are seared into her memory. As a parent, this is where you can make a difference. Having proper conversations makes stronger relationships. Being present makes stronger relationships.

One of the most important times where you can be present is at any school meetings, especially parents' evenings. It is undeniable that a good education is the key that can open many doors for our children especially later in life. We should encourage our young people not to take their access to education for granted. Often, we only realise the importance of education when it is too late.

At one of these events, I saw something that really disturbed me. It was when I attended a year 7 parents' evening for my older daughter and I caught sight of a young girl with her school bag on her back and a notebook in her hand, navigating the desks in the school hall on her own and talking to her teachers. Where were the adults in her life? It shook me that this young girl was on her own taking notes about how she was progressing with the most important part of her life.

I know, in today's economic climate, times are tough for some families and adults are often working more than one job to make ends meet. Time is precious and cannot be discarded easily. But where time is most critical is in school. Children need to see the value that you place on their education by you being at these meetings. If you show that they are important by attending, your child will see the same.

LEARNING

Here are some questions for you to consider:

- Are you giving your child focused attention even if it's for a short time?

- Does your attention depend on their behaviour?

- What are your child's current interests?

- Does your child crave physical touch, conversation, or playing a game?

- Do you give your child your full attention when they need it, even if it disrupts your schedule?

- Are you constantly available, even when they're independently playing?

- Do you rely on screens to keep your child

occupied when you're busy?

- Have you talked to your child about how they feel when they don't get your attention?

Chapter Nine

Present and Active

It is so important teachers know that you as a parent exist in your child's educational life. It can sometimes be the difference in the level of teaching, support, investment and attention your child gets from their teachers.

When Hannah was aged six and in primary school, her school sent out a message to all the parents that her year group would be visiting the Science Museum in central London, and they were inviting parents to attend to support. I decided to go and we had a good time. There were a few lively boys in her class, but I was able to bond with them. I could see that Hannah was so happy to have her dad present. I got to know most of the children in her class and her teacher too.

The thing about primary school is that you stay in the same class with the same students for six years. So, me going on this memorable trip with my daughter fostered a positive relationship with her teacher. But more importantly, I was able to speak and engage with Hannah about her friends in her class for six years. Hannah is 21 years old now and we still speak and have great fond memories about this school trip 15 years down the line.

Hannah had only gotten into trouble once in primary school. The teacher was struggling with the class, and being very studious, Hannah decided to tell off the boys causing disruption. The teacher accused her of policing the classroom. Apparently, she'd done it on a few occasions and the teacher had had enough of her trying to take over his role. Hannah doesn't like anyone disrupting her learning time and always complained about having to sit next to the naughty boys—her words not mine.

On her first day of secondary school, her art teacher tried to make an example of Hannah by telling the whole class that she was going to have a detention the following day for talking. That day, I made sure I left work early as I was intrigued to find out how Hannah's day had gone in "big" school.

'Hannah, how did your first day go?' I asked.

'I actually got in trouble, Dad, and I have a detention after school tomorrow for talking.' Hannah responded.

'Were you talking?' I questioned again.

'No, I wasn't.'

'Don't worry, I understand.' I answered.

And I did. The teacher wanted to make an example of someone to show her new students not to mess around with her. I got it.

But she had picked the wrong child on this occasion. It was around 4.15 pm and I was hoping her teacher was still at school. I called the school and a man with a very posh voice answered the phone.

'Hello, is Ms Smith available?' I asked

The man said, 'Let me look in the staff room to see if she is still here, who should I say is calling?'

'Oh, it's just a parent of one of the new year 7 students.'

The next voice I heard was Hannah's teacher. 'Hello, Ms Smith here.'

I was very nice to her I thought. In a calm voice, I said, 'Hello, Ms Smith. It's Hannah Cato's dad, I would like to talk to you about the detention she is meant to be attending tomorrow.'

Now, I guess on most occasions when Ms Smith picks on a student to hand out the first public detention of the year, she normally selects the right child where the likelihood is their parent won't complain, doesn't care or maybe they're just not present in their child's educational life. I was really interested to know what her selection process was. I mean, why Hannah? Maybe Hannah was having a moment and she was talking when she shouldn't have been, but a detention without a warning? Well, it was evident that Ms Smith did not expect this call and her reply came stumbling out. In a nervous voice she replied 'I'm, ah, so, Hannah's dad, is it? Hello, Mr Cato.'

'Hello, Ms Smith, just wanted to find out why Hannah has to attend a detention tomorrow?'

'Oh, I think there's been a misunderstanding... she doesn't have to, it's all been sorted out now.'

And that was the end of that. Of course, I could have investigated why all of a sudden the detention had been sorted out, but there was no need to. Job done. The teacher knew a parent was present for Hannah and no doubt if her name popped up in the staff room, Ms Smith would be there to pass on the news to the other teachers that Mr Cato was present and active in his daughter's educational life.

Ms Smith and myself got on really well after that. She even tried to persuade me to get Hannah to choose art as one of her options, but Hannah knew exactly what she wanted to choose and unfortunately for Ms Smith, it wasn't art.

I mentioned in a previous chapter that my son, Wesley, had behavioural issues when he was at secondary school. In order for me to keep tabs on him and to show the teachers that I was interested in my son's education, I got all his subject teachers' email addresses. I worked out what the email addresses were from the teachers names on his report. Usually, it's quite simple to do this using the school email address and the name of the subject teacher.

After a not-so-great report that showed Wesley needed to work on a few things, I sent all his subject teachers emails asking for progress updates every two weeks. This had a great impact as I was then able to link rewards to his school progress. This method can really work if you are polite to teachers and they can see that you are doing everything you can to support your child.

I visited an all-boys faith school a few years ago and got speaking to the deputy head, who said the school really struggled getting parents to attend parents' evening, particularly in years 9 & 10. The numbers just seem to drop as the children got older and then picked up again in their last GCSE exam year. He also went on to say poor parent attendance did have a real negative impact on the students' attitudes to learning and behaviour.

I can't emphasise enough the importance of being 100% present in your child's educational life in school and at home. It matters. More than you might realise.

LEARNING

Parents' evenings are so important to attend as they can have a real impact on the educational life of your child. I believe there are some key tips for getting the most out of them.

Top Tips:
- Most schools now have an app that is accessible to parents or an online system for parents to view grades, reports, parent pay, etc. Learn to navigate this system and view it daily.

- Read every email sent from your child's school so you don't miss any event, especially parent evenings.

- Don't wait till the last minute to arrange your meeting(s) with teacher(s). Some of these schools arrange appointments through APPs that can be quite complicated, especially if you have to arrange multiple meetings for different subjects at different times.

- Be on time both in person and online. Once you miss your slot, it's very hard to be seen on the same day.

- Make sure you see your child's report before you meet the teachers as you may want to ask questions about grades, and you don't want any surprises (remember, reports are always sent before parents' evening).

- Be prepared to write or type information down from your meeting with the teacher. This also shows the teachers that you take education seriously and they will take your child seriously and you can address discussion points with your child.

- Try and meet all teachers, not only the subjects you think are the most important like English, Maths and Science. Art and Sports might be important to your child too.

- Always try and find the positives first to feed back to your child and celebrate what is good. Be careful with the language you use when explaining things that are not positive. Use words and phrases like, 'You need to work on...' and 'Try to develop...'

Chapter Ten

Men Don't Talk

1 999 was a crazy year for me. It was the year I became a Christian. In the month of April, I had a 'Paul on the road to Damascus' experience. For those who don't know the story of the Apostle Paul, he totally changed his views about Jesus and Christianity in one day on a journey to Damascus. (Acts Chapter 9 in the Bible).

Yes, my life completely changed in that year and it was definitely for the best.

In December 1999, just a few months as a born-again Christian, I got a call from a friend - Tony Jarrett - who sounded very anxious and worried.

Tony was a 110-metre hurdler. At that time he held the men's English 110-metre hurdles record and had won World, European and Commonwealth medals and participated in the last three Olympics. Tony started explaining to me that he had just got drug tested and the Sample A was showing he had Nandrolone in his system and if the next test, Sample B, showed the same, he would be banned from athletics for a minimum of two years.

Now, everyone has a bit of Nandrolone in their body, however, some athletes take supplements that contain it as it helps them to build muscle and enhance their athletic performance—this is illegal. Tony was devastated and was thinking about his mum being heartbroken if he ever got banned, and his name and career being ruined.

A few months before this conversation on the phone, Tony had told me that he was cooking food in his kitchen when he heard the news on TV that an elite British athlete had failed a drug test. Tony ran straight into the front room where his television set was to see who it was. When the person was revealed, Tony's heart sank as he knew this person and was also taking the same supplements as them.

Tony had a Sports Massage Therapist who had connections with a company that was producing these sports supplements. The therapist introduced Tony to the company's representatives who then explained they had clean, natural supplements and that a couple of the athletes were taking them, including a British elite runner. When they revealed to Tony who the athlete was, Tony knew who he was and already had total respect for this athlete and was sure this person wouldn't be taking any illegal substances, so he started taking the supplements.

When Tony heard the news on the TV, he called the reps from the supplement company straight away and they told him that the athlete must have got "spiked" (when a drug is put into your food or drink without your knowledge) and that they stood by their supplements and reiterated that they were clean. Tony then contacted the British Athletics Association who told him to stop taking the supplements immediately. In the days that followed, more athletes that were taking the same supplements were testing positive.

Tony sounded really shaken down the phone and he kept saying, 'My mum, what is she going to say?' At the time, he was preparing for the European Indoor Championships the following February, then on to the Olympics in the summer. 'This is a disaster, forget this season, it's over,' he continued. I told him not to worry, continue to train and leave it with me for a day or so.

I prayed about the situation, and I believe God told me to get men together to pray for Tony. I asked my mum if I could have the number of her pastor and I was able to contact Pastor Wayne Malcolm. I asked him if I could use one of the rooms in his church to have a prayer meeting for Tony and he was fine about it. I then contacted a few Christian men who I had just got to know and a couple of friends who became Christians before I did. I invited them all to come and pray for my friend, Tony.

It was a Friday night in January 2000 that I will never forget. There was around 15 to 20 men, all from different churches. I didn't really know what I was doing as I was still very green about this Christianity/prayer business. I think I just asked Tony if he wanted to say something, and Tony didn't hold back. He spoke from his heart and let everything out. It was so emotional but so good that he could just be honest like that, and it opened the door for the other men to talk about some of their problems too.

Everything was spoken about that night - from struggles with relationships to issues with finances and health to situations at work to sexual struggles. No one held back. I thought it was going to only be about Tony, but boy was I wrong. It seemed everybody had an issue they wanted to offload. There were tears of hurt, but more importantly, there were tears of joy.

I'd always heard in my life the cliché that 'men don't talk - well, that saying got kicked to the kerb that night because the conversation was amazing.

Never before have I been in an environment where men, most of them hardly knowing each other, felt safe enough to speak openly and honestly about themselves. You could really see the peace and reassurance we were all getting by just opening up to each other. We didn't leave till everybody got individually prayed for. There was a surreal moment when I looked around the room and said to myself, 'This can't stop here, this is just the start.' We left the prayer meeting that night all feeling so contented and encouraged that whatever was to happen next was Gods will.

On the 24th of February 2000, three days before the opening ceremony of the European Indoor championships, Tony was in his Team GB hotel room in Ghent, Belgium with his training partner and friend, Julian Golding. They weren't expecting any visitors, so when the door knocked, Tony's heart started beating like never before.

Tony has been in some high-profile battles on the track with world champions, world record holders, and Olympic gold medallists, including the likes of Colin Jackson, Roger Kingdom, Greg Foster and Allen Johnson, but those were nothing like this battle. This battle was either going to be the beginning of something coming to an end or the beginning of something else, something greater. The biggest battle of his life hung in the balance.

It was Graham Knight, the GB team manager, at the door. 'Jarrett, we have your Sample B results, can you come with me to speak with the team doctors?' Tony couldn't hold back the tears as he went walking to the apartment where the doctors were waiting for him. So many thoughts I'm sure were going through his mind.

'Tony, please come in and sit down. Your results have come back. They are negative, you are clean.' Tony couldn't believe it. He said it was like the whole world just lifted off his shoulders. His first thoughts were, 'Thank you God, my family are not going to be shamed.' The battle was finally won—months of worrying and stressing were over.

When he got back to his hotel room, Tony said to Julian Golding, 'Wow, the prayers of the men.'

From that men's prayer meeting, we all formed a men's group called Men United 4 Christ (MU4C) and it's still helping and supporting men and their families 25 years on.

We run workshops for men and churches, we have held parenting workshops for the community and schools, participated in many events raising money for charities and now run retreats. Our main focus is that we create a safe space for men to talk—Christian or non-Christian, no matter what colour you are or what religion you follow, we are here to support each other, and it works. If men feel safe, men **DO** talk.

I wish every man had an opportunity to have a safe space like MU4C so they can talk about their problems and celebrate their successes, etc. Sometimes I don't feel great within myself and I'm grumpy around the house and towards my family, and a session with the men on Saturday morning just sorts me out.

Just being able to talk out my problems and issues with other men who understand what I'm going through is good enough. Half the time, men don't even need advice about what to do next, they just feel good getting it out. I couldn't tell you how many times this men's group has helped and supported me to be a better dad because they create a non-judgmental environment where men can talk.

It's funny how out of a negative situation something positive can come. Something tells me this is not going to be the only time I say that in this book.

Tony went on to win the bronze medal at this European indoor meeting, and later on that year, ran at his fourth Olympics. He remains one of my closest friends and I love him and his beautiful family dearly.

Men, please talk.

LEARNING

Here are some key points to understand the importance of creating safe spaces for men to talk:

- Challenge Stereotypes: Traditional ideas of masculinity often discourage men from expressing emotions or seeking help.

Safe spaces combat this by showing it's okay to be vulnerable.

- Improve Mental Health: Men have higher suicide rates than women. Talking openly about struggles can be a powerful tool for managing stress, anxiety, and depression.

- Build Stronger Relationships: When men can express themselves freely, it fosters better communication and emotional intimacy in friendships and romantic relationships.

- Reduce Violence: Bottled-up emotions can lead to anger and aggression. Safe spaces allow men to explore healthy ways to deal with difficult feelings.

LEARNING RESOURCES:

- You can find articles and stories about the impact of safe spaces for men as well as mentoring, guidance and support on websites like www.father2father.co.uk

- Websites dedicated to men's health issues like www.uk.movember.com – a male mental health website – which discusses the importance of breaking down stigmas around men's emotions.

- Look for videos or documentaries that explore the experiences of men's support groups on You Tube.

By understanding these benefits, you can become a strong advocate for creating safe spaces for men to talk.

Chapter Eleven

Whose Responsibility Is It?

M en United 4 Christ (MU4C) have led on many parenting sessions and classes. One session we facilitated really sticks out in my mind even though I didn't actually attend. Something came up that day and I couldn't go, but three of the team members were able to run the session and fed back to me.

We ran a session called "Whose Responsibility Is It?" We had five to six parents on each table, and we gave each group a set of 18 small cards and three large cards.

The three larger card headings were:

SCHOOL   HOME   BOTH

The smaller cards had different items on each of them such as how to cook, ironing etc . More examples can be found below in the **LEARNING** section.

The question to the parents was: Whose responsibility is it? Which one of these entities should be teaching your children whatever is on the card?

Each group had to discuss each card and place them under the heading they agreed on. Once the parents put all the cards into categories, there was a wider discussion with all parents in the room about their choices. What was evident with this group of parents was that almost the whole room were in agreement about who should be teaching these things to their children.

The parents thought that 95% of the topics on the cards should be taught by the school and that it was the school's responsibility. We had facilitated this session a few times to different groups, but this was the first time we'd gotten this outcome and also the first time that a group was wholly people of colour – could this be linked in any way?

During the discussion with this group, we broke it down to the parents that if they had the skills to teach these things to their own children before they were taught by the school then there could be a few advantages:

- Give your child a head start/nothing better than learning from your own parents.

- The child will be taught with the values you believe in.

- Some of the subject matters will be good discussion points/build better relationships.

- Parent teaching gives your child another perspective to what the school teaches.

- Your children will teach their children and all of the above will continue.

Also, as schools do not teach many of the topics that were written on the cards, and if you didn't know enough about that particular area, you could speak to other family members or close friends that could then have these discussions with your children instead before they have them at school.

Another concern is, if you don't discuss some of these issues with your child, they might be taught incorrectly by their friends or the internet. It's your responsibility to give your children sound information on key life-learning matters before they are taught in the wrong way, by the wrong person, in an unsafe environment.

The Bible states, 'Children are a gift from God'. Like the educational system, they still belong to us and we don't transfer all responsibilities to anyone. They are still our responsibility, even when we hand them over to someone else to look after.

LEARNING

Let's set you the same task. You can either do this by yourself, with your partner or a group of parents. Use a pencil to mark which category you think each item should come under:

(S – School, H - Home or B -Both)

How to read		Hygiene		How to cook	
Sex Education		Ironing		How to share	
How to open a bank account		Self-Awareness		Organisation skills	
Manners		Counting		Decision making	
Mortgages		Relationships		Alphabet	
Time Management		Nutrition		Financial Literacy	

Here are some questions for you to consider:

- Respect: How can you teach your child to respect themselves, others, and their environment?

- Kindness and Compassion: How can you instil empathy in them and a desire to help others?

- Honesty and Integrity: How can you model honesty and teach the importance of truthfulness?

- Responsibility: How can you give your child age-appropriate responsibilities to foster independence and accountability?

- Resilience: How can you help your child

develop coping mechanisms to bounce back from challenges?

- Communication: How can you encourage clear and confident communication skills?

- Problem-Solving: How can you provide opportunities for your child to develop critical thinking and problem-solving skills?

- Decision-Making: How can you empower your child to make good choices, starting with small decisions?

- Healthy Habits: How can you teach your child healthy eating habits, hygiene, and the importance of exercise?

- Adaptability: How can you help your child adjust to change and new situations?

- Curiosity and Learning: How can you

nurture a love of learning and encourage exploration?

- Gratitude: How can you teach them to appreciate the good things in life?

- Environmental Awareness: How can you instil a sense of responsibility for the environment?

- Digital Citizenship: How can you guide your child in using technology safely and responsibly?

Chapter Twelve

Words Are Powerful

Around the beginning of January 2019, I had a meeting for my extended family at my house and my niece, Rachel, a teenager at the time, suggested the whole family choose an individual "Word of the Year"—this would be a word that carried you through the whole year that you owned and called on any time it was needed. You could study it, research it, etc. but it was yours for the year. We all thought this was a great idea and as soon as she mentioned it, I knew this was something that would stay in my family forever.

My word for the first year was WISDOM and boy, did I need it that year. This word really came through for me as it was one of the most challenging years of my working life. Being a manager and advising head teachers about inclusion isn't an easy job and I had to call on wisdom so many times to make all kinds of decisions. Words are so powerful, and they seem to have even more power if they are written down and not kept in your head. Every year since then, each member of my family writes down their individual Word of the Year.

Right at the beginning of the year, I asked God to give me a word for the year and the word Peace kept on popping into my head. I questioned why because I already felt at peace, nevertheless I went with it. Later on that month, I was diagnosed with a serious illness and I tell you, I really needed that Peace in my life as I got rocked by the news. God truly gave me peace that year and still does. I will tell you a bit more about this story later on in the book.

This year my Word of the Year is SUCCESS.

I was reading a story in the Bible (New King James Version) - Genesis 24 - when Abraham asked his servant to find a wife for his (Abraham's) son, Isaac. In verse 12, the servant prayed,

'O Lord, God of my master Abraham, please give me SUCCESS this day and show kindness to my master Abraham,'. God granted the servant's wish and he found a beautiful woman called Rebecca who became Isaac's wife.

So, the success wasn't really for the servant to benefit, but for him to be successful in order for someone else to benefit – in this case, Abraham's son. I knew straight away that would be my word for the year—SUCCESS.

My sister, Lurine is an international gospel singer, and one year, she decided that her word of the year would be WINNER, and you know what? She was awarded with the Queen's honour of an MBE that year for her services to charity and music, so now we call her Lurine Cato MBE.

I mentioned before that we have two grandchildren. Last year, we gave them their own word for the year. The youngest was given JOY and the older one was given KIND. What was really interesting was that the older one, who is aged four, started reception last year and after the first couple of weeks of him joining, his teacher said to his mum, 'Your son is so kind, he helped a boy who was crying.' Words are truly powerful.

Just before the year ends in December, we start thinking and praying about what word we'll choose for the upcoming year.

I also believe the meaning behind the names you give your children are key too, but that's another topic for another time.

LEARNING

Here are some examples of Words of the Year that you and your family can choose:

'WORD OF THE YEAR' WORD BANK

Successful   Prosperous   Wise   Faith   Confidence   Courage   Resilience   Determine   Forgive   Imagination   Joy   Kindness Opportunity Love   Grace   Believe   Patience   Skill   Value Winner   Beautiful   Miracle   Desire   Success Creative   Peace   Miraculous   Blessed   Bless Stronger   Hope   Progress   Honest   Possible

Wisdom Goodness Knowledge Alive Happy
Integrity Desirable Trust Understanding
Patience

Chapter Thirteen

Adding Value

A few years ago, the Department for Education (DfE) started to judge schools on how much value they added to their young people, our children. They used the children's results from their year 6 test in primary school to make predictions about what they should achieve by the end of year 11 in their GCSEs.

The expectation was that each child should move up a certain number of grades each year. If the young person attained more than these expected grades by year 11, then the school would have had "added value" to the students' progress.

School league tables are often based on these metrics of attainment and progress. I'm not saying

I agree with league tables as a measure of a school's success, but that's just how it is.

So, what can we as parents and family members do to ensure that we add value to our young people so that they not only make the "expected grades" in life but also progress further and achieve above those expectations?

My friend, Bishop Wayne Malcolm (who we fondly call just Bishop), asked my men's group Men United 4 Christ (MU4C), to come together, and spoke to us about a mentoring tool called ARROW, which is an acronym for Aims, Reasons, Reality, Options and Way forward. Bishop made some of his own adaptations to this tool. His tweak came from a Bible scripture - Psalms 127 verses 3 to 5:

3. Children are a heritage from the LORD, off-spring are a reward from him

4. Like arrows in the hands of a warrior are children born in one's youth

5. Blessed is the man whose quiver is full of them. They will not be put to shame when they contend with their opponents in court. (NIV- New International Version)

Bishop described the arrows as our children and that we are blessed when we have many of them (Quiver is full). But also, the arrows in the quiver can be seen as how we direct or aim support for our children and ourselves. The arrow can be used to focus on targets such as:

- Where are you now?

- Where do you want to be in 1/3/5 years' time?

- What do you want to achieve?

- What is your motivation?

- What are your options?

- How are you going to hit your targets?

- What are your first steps?

So, I started using this tool with my nephew, Aaron, who was in his teens at the time and it was seriously amazing. I adapted it so that it worked for him. I remember my first discussion with him being really long and detailed - just going through his aims and what he wanted to achieve for his life.

Getting to know more about my nephew was a real pleasure for me and we had some great discussions about nearly everything - his education, his family, the reality of where he was at that moment in time, where he was in education and about the reasons why he wanted to set and achieve certain goals. The ARROW framework really helped to scaffold the conversation.

We spoke about his GCSE options – both educationally and personally - and I was able to help him with these as well. This entailed talking about his career hopes and ensuring that he opted for subjects that broadly would help him on the path of his choice. I also used **STOP, START, CONTINUE** with him (see chapter one – Changing of a Culture). We used it for education, family relationships and finances. We broke it down into subsections, which gave the framework additional focus.

Following our initial meeting, we agreed to meet four times a year, and from that day to this, it has just continued. We have a brilliant relationship as we have grown together, and we know much more about each other than we otherwise would have. For too many families, the only time they meet is if it is a general occasion i.e. Christmas, weddings, funerals, etc., and often, the conversations are little more than an acknowledgment of our existence.

The ARROW idea really worked. So much so, that I actually brought the concept into my work, and I gave the idea to the mentors in my team, who started using an adapted version of it. It has contributed to some phenomenal things in education in Enfield and is an integral part of our efforts to prevent permanent exclusions.

And it can be just as effective at home. You can use ARROW with your children or your nephews and nieces. It's a great way of building relationships and also getting to know people and them getting to know you in your family. It can give your child or your niece/nephew a framework that they can always go back and refer to.

I recently contacted the original creators Team Improvus and liaised with Jono Elliot, one of the leaders, via email. I wanted to thank him personally for allowing this tool to be used publicly. I really wish I had gathered data on just how many young people have benefitted from this tool.

I highly recommend using it, as it helps illuminate the many ways to add value and it will help you step up from being a standard or below-standard family member to a family member that is more than average. That is when you can add value to your children, to your nephews/nieces, and other family members and friends. It is time to fire some arrows!

For five years, I supported Aaron, my nephew with his goals and his achievements were phenomenal. This experience has given him a solid foundation and a significant part of why he is successful today. But for me, the most important thing was really getting to know him, and him really getting to know me. I am his uncle and he is my nephew, but because of this, we actually became friends. We are still close to this day and that is more important than anything.

LEARNING

Do you want to be graded as a parent/uncle/aunt etc who:

- Is below standard

- Is standard

- Adds value

See below, the completion of the second year I worked with Aaron on ARROW. Feel free to use this framework with your children, family or friends.

Name: Aaron Cato

Date: 05/01/08

A.R.R.O.W – Making Sure you reach your target!

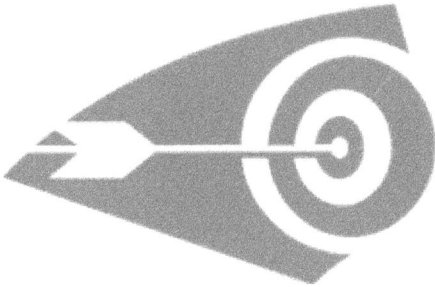

AIMS

1. For this year:

- Become a semi professional footballer – ACHIEVED

- F.A. coaching level 2 – ACHIEVED

- Futsal (an indoors football-based game) Level 1 / Done May 08 – ACHIEVED

- To maintain 11stones weight

- Help my mum destress – ACHIEVED

- Help my sister with her GCSE exams – ACHIEVED

2. For your education/work:

- To get a Distinction/Merit at college – actually achieved Merit/Merit Aug 08 – NOT ACHIEVED

- More work through football/freestyling; adverts, interviews, magazines, websites etc. – ACHIEVED

- To find sponsorship with a company – ACHIEVED

3. **Your Life:**
- To be a professional footballer.

- To go down in history for achieving great things.

- To have my own business – ACHIEVED 08

REALITY

Where are you now compared to where you want to be?

- Playing for Harrow Borough

- Playing National League Futsal

- Playing for England Futsal Team

- Started own coaching business

REASON

Why do you want to achieve your aims?

- I would like to push myself to reach my maximum potential in everything I do.

- Because I enjoy playing football.

- Because I want to earn a living playing football.

- I don't want my mum to work a 9-5.

- I want everyone to know the name Aaron Cato.

- I want to be my own boss.

- I have a good family, and I want to be able to spoil them.

- To go down in history for achieving great things.

- To make my family proud.

<u>OPTIONS</u>

What are the options or routes to your destination? Do you know where you want to go? How are you going to get there?

- Further education

- Weekend job

- Extra football training

- Spend more time with family

- Reading the word daily

- Healthy lifestyle

- Budgeting course

<u>WAY FORWARD</u>

Stop	• Not resting enough* • Putting pressure on myself
Start	• Going to the gym minimum twice a week. • Helping my mum more. • Reading a book. * • Doing more individual football training. • Praying every day. • Talking to people that are close to me more often. • Going to physio when I have an injury. • My own website • Speaking to professionals about starting own business • Business cards • Register business
Continue	• Asking people for advice • Getting an education. • Being independent. • Coaching at Tottenham Hotspurs. • Playing football, training, practising. • Giving Lauren (sister) advice. • Making more money. • Getting more work through freestyling. • Praying. • Promoting myself. • Being humble.

* Needs to be achieved by next review

** Not achieved at last review. Has to be achieved by next review

How well do you think you are doing at the moment in the following areas? Rate your self out of 10 marks i.e.   1 = poor / 5 = satisfactory / 10 = brilliant.

Date: 05/01/08

Health	College	Relationship with Family	Work	Financial Status	Football
9	8	8	8	8	7

Date: 03/04/08

Health	College	Relationship with Family	Work	Financial Status	Football
9	6	5	9	9	5

Date: 05/07/08

Health	College	Relationship with Family	Work	Financial Status	Football
7*	8	7	9	9	7

Eyes 2yrs ago ; Dentist 2yrs ago

Date:15/10/08

Health	College	Relationship with Family	Work	Financial Status	Football
4	5	8	8	9	8

Date: 05/01/09

Health	College	Relationship with Family	Work	Financial Status	Football
4	0	8	8	5	8

Aaron's 2008 Review

This year, through being more focused and less distracted, I have completed a vast amount of my goals. Passing my FA coaching level 2 was very big for me because I felt that I deserved to be a level 2 coach a long time ago. Also, passing my level 1 in Futsal coaching made me proud of myself as I could now be taken more seriously because of qualifications.

My freestyle work and private coaching picked up in a massive way, and through this, I started my own business. Playing my first game for England Futsal squad made me hold my head up high because I knew that I had been chosen for my ability, and my hard work felt valued.

I would like to dedicate the year to my mum because she has done so much for me and kept me strong, and she never doubted anything I said I was going to do even if it seemed risky.

Chapter Fourteen

Helena Already Knows

The more secrets you have about you or your family, the more dangerous it gets as your children grow up. Why do I say dangerous? I would like to think most of the time children grow up holding their parents and grandparents in high esteem no matter how much grief they might have given us. Children can find things out by accident - at funerals, family holidays, reunions or from gossipers or people who are just jealous of your family.

We love our older generation, but as they get older, they can sometimes lose their verbal filter and believe they can say anything to anyone. I've heard stories of people visiting older relatives back in their parents' home country and coming back with shocking news they previously didn't know about.

Even I've been surprised like that a few times. I don't blame my parents at all though, it's just sometimes things are not said and you kind of have to work it out yourself, but when you have worked it out, it's either, you just don't feel like you can speak to them about certain sensitive issues, or it's too late because they are not around anymore.

Sometimes you can find out something but it hasn't been delivered in the right way, so it can bring about hurt and resentment – after all, what family doesn't have secrets? The problem is, whilst I think my generation are tough enough to handle unexpected news and secrets that just come out of the blue, I'm not so sure if the next generation have the resilience or emotional intelligence to deal with such news.

It is often said that young people today have to deal with more stress and pressure now than ever before. Then add all the information and content from social media... well, that takes it to another level. Since Facebook was introduced to this world, how many secrets have been exposed via this platform and damaged families? In order to protect your children and your relationships with them, expose the secrets yourself in a safe way, so as to minimise any possible fallout. There is nothing worse than hearing family secrets from other people that aren't your immediate family.

But when is the right time to tell your children sensitive news that might rock their world a little bit? It all depends on the level of the information and the way your child processes and deals with information. As a parent, you would be in the best position to know this. It's always good to test your children with different levels of information.

When I was younger, I led a very colourful life. My dad had 18 children, and as I mentioned before, 11 of them were with my mum and the other seven were with other women. So, what I'm trying to say is that I believe I inherited certain traits from my dad, and by the time I reached the age of 14-15,

I realised I wasn't a bad-looking young man. As you can see, I am trying to pick my words carefully. I led a very exciting teenage life, which continued into my late 20s.

I've mentioned in recent chapters about **Life Long Learning.** Well, in this period, I certainly did learn! My friends and I were having lots of fun, but it was at a cost and so many things in my past have unfortunately come back to bite me. However, I made sure I told my children all about their dad's youthful days, running around with my friends and their uncles, causing mayhem.

My children love hearing some of my stories as I made sure they were delivered in an engaging way but also explaining the downsides and the repercussions I faced due to the wrong decisions I made.

My family have always lived in Enfield, London, so you can imagine with a very big family of 11 kids growing up together, my family's name was well known in the local community and neighbouring boroughs. Thank God my wife didn't know too much about me before we married. She grew up in a completely different circle of people—I truly do thank God for that.

When we got married and she had to change her surname, boy did things change for her overnight. From the banks to the Post Office to the kids' school...simply everywhere. Whenever she had to mention her full name - Sophia Cato - she was questioned, 'How are you related?' 'Which Cato are you married to?' and so on and so on, and believe me, it wasn't always nice stories for her. But because I had given Sophia a "heads up" beforehand and all secrets were on the table, it made things much easier for her... well, maybe just a little bit easier! Even how many years down the line, every so often Sophia will still experience similar moments, but she is used to it now and just takes it in her stride.

Just before the Lockdown, Hannah, my daughter, aged 17 at the time, was coming back from the gym on the bus and overheard two women talking about me. This was years after I'd calmed down my colourful ways, was happily married, a Christian and generally settled into my model citizen role in life. However, these ladies were talking about my past years, and they were really going "in". My daughter said she found it so funny, this new remixed version of my life was hilarious to her and she didn't want to get off the bus, but would have missed her stop if she'd stayed to listen on.

When I came home that evening, both my daughters were laughing as Hannah didn't waste any time telling her younger sister, Helena, what she had heard on the bus. Hannah said, 'If only those women knew who was sitting behind them.' You see, we could all laugh about it as I had already told my daughters about me, and so my past wasn't a secret to them.

Sophia and I decided years ago to tell all our children all the family "stuff" to make sure they were not vulnerable to hearing anything about our past life that might unsettle them. What was interesting was that as we were revealing stories to them, they were saying they already knew most of them!

Just recently, Sophia and Helena attended a funeral and someone said something to Helena about her grandfather, Sophia's father, not in a malicious way, but they caught themselves and put their hand over their mouth as if to say, 'I shouldn't have said that.' but Sophia just smiled and said, 'Don't worry, **Helena already knows**.'

So, try to leave no stone unturned when it comes to informing your children about 'family stuff', and remember, it doesn't matter how bad the news is, if it doesn't come from you, just imagine how much worse it could be coming from someone else. Remember, open and honest communication is key. By creating a safe space for dialogue, you can help your child process family secrets in a healthy, positive way.

RESOURCES

Websites:

- The National Society for the Prevention of Cruelty to Children (NSPCC): This UK-based charity offers a great resource on difficult conversations with children, including tips on starting the conversation, age-appropriate language, and safety considerations.

- One Family: This Irish organization provides guidance on communicating with your child about family secrets, particularly regarding adoption or family history.

Books:
- "How to Talk So Kids Will Listen & Listen So Kids Will Talk" by Adele Faber and Elaine Mazlish: This classic parenting book offers practical tips on communication with children of all ages, including techniques for handling difficult conversations [Title: How to Talk So Kids Will Listen & Listen So Kids Will Talk].

Articles:
- "Parenting | Communicating with Your Child about Family 'Secrets'" by One Family: This article delves into why secrets can be harmful and offers strategies for open communication with your child.

Additional Tips:

- Consider your child's age and maturity level: Tailor the conversation to what they can understand and process.

- Focus on honesty and age-appropriate language: Be truthful but avoid over-whelming details.

- Create a safe space for questions and reassurance: Let your child know they can ask anything and express their feelings openly.

- Be prepared for emotional responses: Family secrets can evoke a range of emotions. Be patient and supportive.

- Seek professional help if needed: If the conversation is particularly difficult or the secret involves abuse or trauma, consider consulting a therapist or counsellor who specializes in family communication.

Chapter Fifteen

Where There's a Will There's a Way

There is something that is really close to my heart and I have really thought about whether I should mention it in this book. I decided that I have to because I have seen many families break up because of this very reason.

When parents pass away, the children they leave behind are most of the time grieving and very often have to pick up the pieces and start sorting out funeral arrangements when they are still in an emotional state. Often, if siblings are involved, sometimes things can get heated, and I've seen even the most easy-going of people fall out with their siblings during this period.

Our family went through a difficult time when our father passed away as he didn't have any funeral plans written down. However, it went very smoothly when our mum passed away, as everything was written down and there was no way we were going to make the same mistake twice.

If you really want to make things easier for your children, please organise your funeral. Write it down and make sure your family know your wishes. That is not the only thing I would like to advise. I also recommend when your children are old enough that you tell them about your will.

Yes, I said your will.

Think about it... parents pass away, children are grieving *and* arranging a funeral. Then whilst they are all still in a highly emotional state, they are told what is being left to them or find out what is *not* being left to them. With so much happening in a potentially short space of time, it's no wonder so many brothers and sisters fall out with each other at a time when they should be supporting each other.

Wills that are only revealed after death could be one of the riskiest secrets of all, as sometimes the only person that can keep the peace and mediate is the one that has just passed away. Naturally, there are also cons to revealing a will before parent(s) pass away, but that is one of the things that in my humble opinion, needs to be weighed up. I would like to believe that *most* people (as one can't really swear for everyone!) aren't hatching some sort of sinister plan to 'top' off their parents for an inheritance payday!

I realise this topic is a matter of opinion and tradition, but my wife and I made a decision to tell our children the contents of our will a few years ago and they were cool with it. We will remind them again when we feel we might need to hopefully far into the distant future, but we're hoping that our children, Wesley, Hannah and Helena will remain close as siblings when that time comes. More importantly that they stay friends.

Chapter Sixteen

Canada Geese

My dad, may God bless his soul, passed away a few years ago, but when he was alive, he had issues with his prostate, so I used to have annual check-ups. Due to the lockdown, I didn't have any tests during this period. In December 2022, I was in Edmonton Green in Enfield and saw my brother-in-law who was explaining to me the issues he was going through regarding his prostate. He was urging me to go and get tested. As soon as he mentioned it, I knew that I had to go and get tested again.

So, I went and had a PSA blood test and was told I needed to get an MRI scan. After the MRI scan, they didn't give me my results but referred me for a biopsy, which I might add, wasn't pleasant at all. I then received a letter in the post with an appointment to meet the Urologist. This set off little alarm bells inside me as previously when I had gotten tested, I got the results over the phone and that was that.

Sophia came with me to the appointment for support, and as we sat in the waiting room, I was really nervous. It seemed like the longest wait ever but, finally, my name was called. As soon as we walked into the room, I could tell by the doctor's face it wasn't going to be good news and, sadly it wasn't. He explained that cancer had been found in my prostate. Sophia took a hold of my hand and squeezed it for support, the rest of what the Urologist said was a blur as my heart sank after the word "cancer". I couldn't process anything else.

What's strange is whenever you hear about cancer, most things you listen to on the radio or what you see on TV is nearly always about someone dying from it and obviously the thought of that didn't help. I do believe that when people get this type of news, particularly men, it can often lead to depression – so much so, it feels like that the news of the cancer alone can potentially lead to their life ending earlier than the actual cancer itself. Well, I was determined that wasn't going to happen to me.

Firstly, I made some adjustments to my diet. Then, to help with my emotional wellbeing, I removed myself from all WhatsApp groups that weren't edifying. I was more conscious about what I was watching on TV – violent and negative programs and films were removed from my binge list. Even the conversations I was having with people had to be either educational or enriching in some way. I just knew I needed to stay positive from all angles, and I think God was putting me through a season of cleansing. A time to rethink everything.

I shared my diagnosis with all my extended family and asked them all to pray for me, and their support was amazing. I think I've got the best family in the world. Do we always get on? Most certainly not, but if ever I'm down and need a pit stop, they are there to refuel me and fix me up to go again. Remember that support team I mentioned in Chapter 6 F1 experience? It's a great idea for adults too, especially in testing times.

I asked the Christian men's group, Men United 4 Christ, to pray for me and urged them to also get tested, and thankfully some of them did. What a support these guys are! I informed my pastor, and she had the whole church praying for me and my family. The support I received from everyone was overwhelming. I have some wonderful friends and when they heard my news, well, they wouldn't leave me alone! But in a good way. With regards to support, they are always there for me and my family. Even my team at work decided to give me less stress—only joking lol, but they are a lovely set of people and I'm blessed to work with them.

Over the next few months, since my diagnosis in January, I had more good days than bad days, from the lockdown, Sophia and I stopped going to church, as did many people, but we, didn't really go back even after the lockdown ended. So, emotionally and spiritually, we weren't in the best place. I was tired all the time and simply felt that l didn't have the energy to lead anymore. And so,

I just didn't want to. I'd always believed that the man should lead the family as my dad was very much a man's man and I was strongly influenced by him. Even though I could see with my eyes, that my mum was the quiet leader in the background, I'd always seen a man at the front. Now, I was going through a season of not wanting to be at the front, and in a way, so was Sophia. She was tired too and had her own issues, not just with supporting me but also caring for her mum as well. It was a strange time.

Have you ever looked up in the sky and seen a flock of birds flying in an arrowhead formation or a V formation? Well, those are called Canada Geese. I always wondered why they flew like that, so I did some research and found they do this for many reasons.

First, it conserves their energy. Each bird flies slightly above the bird in front of them, resulting in a reduction of wind resistance. The birds take turns being in the front, falling back when they get tired, and another bird takes the lead. In this way, the geese can fly for a long time before they need to stop for rest.

What was amazing was in my flock, the baby of the family, Helena, at the age of 16 stepped up to the front and took the lead. Nobody asked her to, nobody forced her to, she just turned into this leader and showed qualities I really didn't know she possessed. Helena challenged Sophia and I about our faith and beliefs and invited us to go to her church, Jubilee Enfield. Prior to that, we hadn't been regularly going to church for over 18 months.

The second benefit of the V formation is that it is easy to keep track of every bird in the group. Flying in formation assists with the communication and coordination within the group. Fighter pilots often use this formation for the same reason. Helena was keeping track of her parents and realised something was wrong—that something was missing from our lives.

I believe that you can learn and develop from any life experience if you are open minded enough and willing to "see". You can dwell in the negativity when things get tough, but it is often these times when the greatest learning opportunities occur if you look for them. On this occasion, something so negative produced something so positive. Some great leaders are born out of adversity.

There is so much I could say about how Helena took charge, but she is a very quiet, humble person who never likes a fuss being made of her – she just...did what she felt needed to be done for our family to get our groove back. It goes to show that if you put in the work with your children from the start, you will see the fruits flourish...and wow is she flourishing.

This book is about the whole family and Hannah, my eldest daughter, on many occasions has also taken the lead. I didn't really recognise it at the time until I reflected on the many occasions when she has organised, arranged and taken charge too. Always quietly and confidently, time after time, she has been that consistent young woman who so many people look up to and depend on for the practical things that need doing. In her turn,

Hannah never looks down on anyone, she is very precise and intelligent in her doings and yet so humble.

Wesley also had to become a man very quickly and he mirrored my life in so many ways. However, he adjusted to fatherhood much earlier and better than I did. He has joined his children in our V formation so smoothly and I commend him for that. He is more resilient than he gives himself credit for. I'm truly proud of him. He is also a believer in the three Ls—Life-Long Learning—and because of this, he is and will continue to be a great leader. It's funny, from the time he was born, my mother always called him The Great Man Wesley. Words are truly powerful, there's life and death in the power of the tongue, and my mother, God bless her soul, definitely spoke life saying that.

I can't thank God enough for blessing me with a wonderful family, a flock of leaders, but ultimately, God is always at the helm of our family and all things are possible with him.

LEARNING

Tips:

- Lead by Example: Children are constantly observing and mimicking the adults around them. Be a role model who demonstrates good leadership qualities like honesty, integrity, empathy, and resilience.

- Empower Through Choice: Give your child opportunities to make choices, even small ones. This builds confidence and allows them to practice decision-making skills.

- Encourage Teamwork: Activities like sports teams, clubs, or group projects help children learn collaboration, communication, and how to work towards a common goal.

- Foster Responsibility: Assign age-appropriate chores and hold them accountable for completing them. This instils a sense of responsibility and ownership.

- Embrace Mistakes as Learning Opportunities: When your child makes a mistake, use it as a chance to teach them problem-solving skills and the importance of perseverance.

- Provide Opportunities to Lead: Look for ways your child can take charge in different situations. Maybe they can help plan a family outing or lead a game with friends.

- Develop Communication Skills: Help your child express themselves clearly and confidently. Encourage them to listen actively to others and communicate their ideas respectfully.

- Celebrate Effort and Progress: While achievement is rewarding, acknowledge the effort and dedication your child puts into their endeavours. This fosters a growth mindset and intrinsic motivation.

- Teach Empathy and Compassion: Help your child understand the perspectives and feelings of others. Encourage acts of kindness and service to the community.

- Provide Challenges: Don't shield your child from all difficulties. Let them face age-appropriate challenges that allow them to develop problem-solving skills and resourcefulness.

- Be a Supportive Coach: Offer guidance and encouragement but allow your child to take ownership of their actions and decisions. Be there to celebrate their successes and help them learn from setbacks.

Remember, leadership development is a journey, not a destination. By providing a supportive and enriching environment, you can help your child blossom into a confident and inspiring leader who is ready to take their turn at the front just like the Canada Geese.

Chapter Seventeen

The Bigger Picture

Psalm 128

A song of ascents.

¹ Blessed are all who fear the Lord,   who walk in obedience to him.

² You will eat the fruit of your labor;   blessings and prosperity will be yours.

³ Your wife will be like a fruitful vine   within your house;your children will be like olive shoots around your table.

⁴ Yes, this will be the blessing   for the man who fears the Lord.

⁵ May the Lord bless you from Zion;   may you see the prosperity of Jerusalem   all the days of your life.

[6] May you live to see your children's children—peace be on Israel. (NIV – New International Version)

I have been reading and praying this scripture over my family since I married Sophia, which is before Hannah, Helena and our grandchildren were born. I've mentioned before how powerful words can be, especially when they are spoken out loud. In the bible, Proverbs 18 verse 21 says, "…the tongue has the power of life and death, and those who love it will eat its fruit (NIV)." Psalms 128 is one of my favourite scriptures. My advice for you is to find a scripture for your family, read it out weekly and believe and have faith that it will come to pass.

I do have an ideal plan of how I want my family to be. There is nothing wrong with having an idea of what you want the bigger picture to look like for your family. I believe the principles below are working towards the bigger picture I want for my family and hopefully for yours:

- That we, and our children and their children will love the Lord our God with all our hearts and with all our souls and with all our strength and with all our minds and, last of all, love our neighbour as we would love ourselves.

- For our family to live together in unity with open and honest systems in place to resolve any issues that might cause division.

- For all of our children to go through our Rites of Passage to give them a firm foundation before becoming an adult.

- For our family to live together on a large family plot with multiple separate homes so our young people will be mortgage-free and financially able to help other people, and to live a stress-free life so they can live their dreams and fulfil their God-given purpose.

- For our family to form a wider family organisation that supports financial growth for our family so it can impact our community and make it flourish.

So, the decision my mum made when I was 19 to walk away and say nothing to me or anyone else about what she saw that day was strategic—a tactical move to hopefully make me take note of my future. She didn't gossip, didn't complain, and knowing my mum, she just took it to God and left it with him as he always sees the bigger picture. Job done, Mum; I will always love you.

Chapter Eighteen

A Word From My Parenting Mentor

D ear Parent,

I don't know where you may find your-self within the landscape of parenting. Whether you are a young parent faced with the prospect of having your very first child, or whether you are a mature grandparent, possibly great grandparent several times over.

In my time as a family practitioner one of the greatest abilities any parent can ever possess, is the ability to reflect on one's own style of parenting and recognise the impact it has or continue to have on children you are responsible for.

The term '*reflects*' or '*self-reflection*' means:

"The activity of thinking (deeply) about one's own feelings and behaviours, and the reasons that may lie behind one's actions."

In other words, reflection is the art of critically looking at the way in which you have parented your children and honestly recognising parenting decisions and behaviours you could have done differently that would have enabled greater positive outcomes for your children. Reflection is also the genuine desire and ability to actively implement change in your own behaviour.

I always liken a new-born baby to a 'blank canvas' on which we the parent has the responsibility/artistic license to produce a Rembrandt quality image.

Question: Are you happy with the way in which your blank canvas has turned out?

For those who are currently in the parenting arena; whether this be raising toddlers through to adolescences, or whether you are navigating your children through the rapids we refer to as teenager years, or at the stage where your children are now parenting their own children. Wherever you may find yourself; the question that remains is, "What could I have done differently to allow for a better outcome?" Followed by the motivational strategies and humility to 'CHANGE'.

My experience has shown that many people, due to mental, emotional, or neurodiverse factors, struggle with self-awareness and the ability to accurately critique their own behaviour. This can hinder their understanding of their role in parent-child or co-parenting relationships. Despite a genuine desire to improve, they may find it difficult to change their own behaviour for the benefit of their children, spouse, or family.

Despite these challenges, it's important to remember that change is possible. With the right support, individuals can develop self-awareness, learn new coping mechanisms, and improve their relationships. By seeking help from therapists, counsellors, or support groups, people can gain valuable insights and tools to foster healthier interactions with their loved ones. It's a journey that may require time and effort, but the rewards—stronger relationships, greater personal fulfilment, and a more positive family environ-ment—are well worth the investment.

Robert George, Retired Family Worker

Acknowledgements

Exceptional Thanks

First and foremost - To my God who found me when I was so lost, blessed me with an amazing wife and family and gave me a purpose, something I didn't have before, and without Him, I don't know where I would be.

Heartfelt Thanks

Maria Amartey nee Lewis who has been guiding me all the way through this process, your experience and support has been immense. Thank you so much for your encouragement and your endless patience. How you kept your hands from circling my neck is indeed a miracle!

Thank you to James Carrick for helping me write this book. I have enjoyed every moment of putting this together and having wonderful discussions with you during our times together.

Big thanks to Stuart Lawrence, Richard Kelly, Simon Elliott and Ayse Adil for giving me constructive feedback on this book.

Matt Bird for dropping that seed to encourage me to write this book.

Thank you Karen Allen for giving me guidance.

Special Thanks

To my wonderful brothers and sisters, all your support throughout the years has been immense.

To my mother-in-law and father-in-law for always being present and there for our children.

To my brothers-in-law and sisters-in-law, you have been so supportive to me and my family, you are truly family too.

To Above The Clouds for changing the family landscape - the best is yet to come!

To my uncle and aunties, past and present, for all the great principles you have poured into me.

To my cousins who I have shared wonderful fun times with.

To my friends, you know who you are. You are amazing people that have consistently supported me and my family.

To Men United 4 Christ, our relationships are amazing. You guys mean so much to me, your partners have been a massive support - God bless you all.

To the F.I.R.E group, your prayers have opened so many doors. You guys are great.

To K.I.C.C The Lighthouse Church, my family owe so much to you and your families.

To Father 2 Father – Courtney, you and your team have done fantastic work in our community for men and their families.

Colin & Dee Eimer for showing me a different way.

SBSS for being a wonderful set of people to manage.

To The Hope Givers, you are an awesome set of men that are a beacon for our community and beyond.

Jubilee Church, my new family.

To Mr & Mrs Kelly, thank you for all the support you continue to give me.

To the Morris family, we are family.

Individual Thanks

For these people I mention, you know the reasons why I have so much love for you:

Sister Annette

Pastor Trevlyn

Angela Thomas

Liselle Archer

Darren & Tracey Harrison

Jason Small

Marc Anthony

Patrick Marshall

Junior Henry

Marie Sutherland

Justin Cochrane

Courtney & Lois Brown

Bishop Wayne Malcolm

Sharon Cato

Rosemary Cato

Simonette Sehindemi

Jo Fear

Olivia Wittich

Alex Saran

Diane Anderson

Robert George

Laverne Antrobus

Carol Mighty

Yvonne Black

Rudolph Walker CBE

Sarah Eckert

Trevor Radway

Pastor Geoffrey Folkes

Jonathan Etuk

Dionne John

Diane Parrish

Jennifer Rankin

Tony & Bev Jarrett

Eddie (My Barber)

Rio Maclaren

And last but definitely not least - thank YOU for reading this book. I hope it will have a positive impact on you and your family.

About The Author

Mervin Cato isn't just an educationalist; he's a seasoned father of three children navigating the wild world of parenthood alongside his wife, Sophia. He also has two energetic grandchildren who are full of life.

With over 20 years spent in the trenches—working in the school educational system and then directly with local authorities - Mervin brings a unique blend of academic expertise and real-life experience to the table. His team was instrumental in reducing permanent exclusions in his local authority by 80% and making them one of the lowest permanent excluding boroughs in London and one of the top 20 lowest boroughs nationally. In 2022, Mervin managed a team that won a national award for delivering better outcomes for young people in the local authority he works for.

His passion for community and inclusion extends far beyond textbooks. He believes that the most important lessons happen at home, and that nurturing strong parent-child relationships is the foundation for a child's success.

Through years of juggling homework battles, bedtime negotiations, and chairing lively family meetings, Mervin has developed a practical approach to parenting that focuses on fostering communication, building confidence, changing culture and celebrating the joys (and inevitable messes) that come with raising a family.

As one of 11 children, Mervin has grown from being a negative teen roaming the streets of North London to being a proactive man pushing to affect positive change in his community.

This book is a culmination of his experiences—in education, the community and at home. It's a resource for parents who want to navigate the exciting, challenging, and ultimately rewarding journey of raising happy, well-adjusted children.